DEBBY HAVAS

MY JOURNEY
TO WHOLENESS

Nature and a healing presence restored her

MY JOURNEY TO WHOLENESS

Published by Deborah D. Havas; Jay, New York. All rights reserved.
For permission to quote or reprint contact: ddh46er@yahoo.com

Library of Congress Cataloging-in-Publication Data
Applied for

ISBN: 978-0-69273-487-2

Printed in the United States of America

page 265: "Greatest Love of All" *lyrics by Linda Creed,*
music by Michael Masser, produced by Michael Masser

page 267: "Hero" *written and produced by*
Mariah Carey and Walter Afanasieff

Design: Peter Gloege | LOOK Design Studio

Editorial development and creative design support by Ascent:
www.itsyourlifebethere.com

for my brother, Bud, in loving memory
I knew you were always 'there' for me
you were my model in my growing years
you have been my hero my entire life

for Gary, my best friend and soul mate
you opened the door and set my soul free
you have shown me true love
and for that I am forever grateful

CONTENTS

TO MY READERS

I was given the following in high school, and it has become a philosophy I have tried to live by for my entire life. May it be as great a guide for you as it has been for me.

> *God grant me the serenity*
> *To accept the things I cannot change;*
> *The courage to change the things I can;*
> *And the wisdom to know the difference.*
> *—Reinhold Neibuhr*

Much of my story has come from my personal journals which I have kept since the day I was diagnosed. They have been a great resource for writing this manuscript. Since this is a memoire, I have changed some of the names of the characters in my story to protect their privacy. The story line takes place over twenty years ago. We were all different people back then.

We have learned.

We have grown.

We have evolved.

INTRODUCTION

*I have often wished to write a book and have thought
of children's stories or a character I would create in my mind.
The desire is strong now. The character is me.
Years ago, I never would have guessed that, with pen on page,
it would be My story. And so I now begin, trusting that
in some way, someone, someday will be touched by
His hand through this expression of His love for me.*

—TAKEN FROM MY PERSONAL JOURNAL, JULY 2, 1987

Have you ever asked yourself, "Why am I here? What is my purpose? What am I supposed to learn from this?" Let's think about it. We get ill. We get well. We focus on the "cure". But what about our journey? It is in the *journey* that we find our opportunity to get it together for once. We can begin to find answers to some of these same questions we've been asking ourselves our entire lives.

A challenging life experience can show us the way, sometimes jump starting us, leading us to a new perspective and providing us with the opportunity to grow and heal emotionally, physically and spiritually. That has happened to me.

I have grown through a challenging experience that came catapulting into my life. I had no way of knowing what the culmination would be. I had no way of knowing what choices would be presented to me along the way nor the decisions required of me as I sought to endure my journey. I had been placed in a situation which I couldn't control, couldn't plan and couldn't organize. The need to do so had become, for me, a way of life.

When did all this happen? *How* did all this happen? *Why* did all this happen?

I opened myself up to the journey, one of awareness and choice, and in so doing I have discovered more of who I am and my purpose in life. I have learned SO much...

THIS IS MY SONG.

PROLOGUE

It's 9:00 in the morning. I am standing rigidly at my kitchen sink, listening to the drip, drip, drip of the water leaking from the faucet in front of me. My bare feet are rooted to the icy cold floor. I stare out the misty window at the landscape I so love—majestic mountains, trees with lofty branches, the mottled sky—feeling the quiet calm reassurance of Nature, that all of this is of purpose. I have the sense that there *is* a purpose, a greater plan for everything.

Yet I don't feel I have purpose anymore, if I ever did. Nor do I have the energy to strive and discover and pursue whatever purpose I may have. At a basic level, that requires me to still believe I am here on earth for a reason. And . . . I just don't know.

The truth is, I feel like I am drowning, going down for the third time, and this time there may be no coming back up, no gasp of air as I resurface, no return. Though I reach upward, I am fading . . . fading . . . fading away from the light so far distant at the surface.

I can see through the water as I sink to the depths—down . . . down . . . down. My stomach is totally wound like a knot pulled tight as my saddened heart feels the agony of my existence.

I feel the weakness of my leg muscles, barely supporting this body in an upright position. My legs begin to quiver as if soon they will no longer keep me vertical at all. I grip the edge of the sink so tightly my knuckles turn white and my breath comes labored in short gasps.

My gaze shifts to my left where a set of knives hangs on the side of a cabinet, so stately and secure in its wooden home. Each has its place in the holder. Each fits just right. *Where is* my *place? I don't seem to fit anywhere.*

I stare at the knives as if they hold a deep secret. I wonder . . . *do I remove the sharpest one and sever the veins in my wrist? Could I really do that? I so want an end to my long endured pain.* Moments pass as I stand there becoming weaker and weaker.

In another moment an image flashes through my mind. *My girls. I can't do what my mind is tempting. They would always feel that in some way, they were to blame. I cannot burden them with that. I must endure the loneliness I feel, not from my girls but in my marriage. I need to feel loved and understood, shown some compassion. Instead, I am receiving nothing, nothing at all.*

I turn away from the sink, away from the knives, away from my thoughts. I leave the kitchen and move slowly down the hallway, feeling the comforting softness of the carpet beneath my feet. I enter the bedroom where I stop for a moment, staring at the blue design on the quilt, a huge pointed star.

Stars . . . I'm amazed at the universe out there. What a contrast to my previous thoughts. *I love a blackened night sky spangled with pulsing sparkling stars. This is who I really am, a woman in love with the natural world of twinkling starry skies, flower buds bursting with promise, fragrant evergreen trees, swirling meandering streams and rising mountain peaks.*

How did I become so drained of life? What did this to me? It feels as if someone has been pulling the plug at the bottom of my soul for most of my life, always pulling me down when I want to rise. But when did this begin? And how, if possible, can I change the fact that I have abandoned, over and over again, my own life . . . my one precious life, to satisfy the wills and for the sakes of, others?

I lower my body to the bed. I feel so drained, so tired.

As I sit there at the edge of the quilt, running my hand over the perfectly stitched patches, I realize that I can never tell anyone about today, that I even *considered* taking my own life. It's against my religion. I know that no one in my family or any of my friends ever thought of doing that. I feel ashamed, ashamed that I felt so 'at the end of it'. But I DID. I can't see . . . I can't see where this all leads. And there are my girls, always my girls.

I lie back on the bed and stare at the white lumpy ceiling, my pillow resting snuggly beneath my head. As I pull the blue blanket over my frigid body, my eyes begin to close. My mind drifts to thoughts of my mother. *How did you do it, Mom? How did you possibly live through those years of my birth and afterwards? How did you survive? Tell me. Please, tell me . . .*

My mind continues to drift through time. I can see myself lying in that bed with the blue blanket pulled up over me like I am in a cocoon, awaiting my metamorphosis. I can even feel like I did then. The desolation and aloneness I experienced had housed itself in every fiber of my being, and it was still there with me so many years later, festering like a low-grade infection.

I gradually become aware of a soft gentle voice that is beginning to ease itself into my mind, my consciousness. It calls to me. I'm being led and I *want* to follow.

"I want you to take a deep breath, Debby, as you come back to present time, slowly inhaling and filling your lungs with air. That's it . . . deeply . . . fully. Now, even more slowly, begin to release the air. Feel it flow out of you, gently leaving your lungs. As you release the air, release the shame, the guilt you have carried all these years," Rebecca says, speaking with compassion.

I find myself here with a woman called Rebecca. It is *her* voice that is leading me. It is *her* voice that I am following. We are here in her small, wooden home in the rural Adirondack Mountains of New York. The space is quiet and comforting. I am able to easily share with her. I feel accepted by her, and her compassion speaks loudly to me, encircling me, holding me there like a safety net. I realize I've been speaking my tale to her, reliving those moments in my past, a time of trauma. She is gently guiding me through a mode of relaxation and self-forgiveness. I so want to understand myself and feel better, really better.

I continue breathing and releasing for a time, consciously willing the guilt and shame to vacate my soul, guilt that I had even considered taking my own life. And shame that I had only considered what that would have done to my girls as a *second* thought. Slowly . . . slowly . . . slowly . . .

"Now take another slow breath, inhaling deeply from your belly," Rebecca continues. "Notice how full your lungs are beginning to feel. Focus on the air filling you as your lungs expand. When you're ready, begin the exhale, even slower than your inhale has been. Continue to breathe deeply and, little by little, allow the air to escape and take with it any hurts you may have encountered surrounding this emotional episode."

Again, I focus on her suggestion in releasing the hurt, trying to attach myself to that moment of desperation in my marriage that had brought me to this point, at this space in time. Breath after breath, the minutes pass.

"Let it go . . . Let it go . . . ," she says in a whispered voice. I feel the tenseness dissipate, my muscles begin to relax, my mind quiets, and my thought stills.

Softly, ever so softly, I again hear her voice. "Another deep breath, from the belly, welcoming into your consciousness *new* understanding, *new* insights, *new* positive energies. As you very slowly exhale, release anything that no longer serves you."

Inhaling, I welcome newness into my life. That is what I desire—new perspective, yet, an understanding of the past. Exhaling, I release the anger, the hurt, the resentment toward my husband. I feel it lessen as moments pass. Still, it's not *all* gone. I recognize that I need to forgive the past, if that is possible. I'm not sure, but maybe. *Lead me, Father. Lead me. Give me the energies to try again.*

I hear the return of Rebecca's voice, offering an invitation. "You may open your eyes now, Debby." I allow a few moments to pass.

I realize I am very relaxed and not altogether with it. I feel a little groggy, like I've been on a trip somewhere else. As I sit there, I become more and more alert.

"How do you feel?" Rebecca asks.

"I feel a great relief—like I've cast a burden off my shoulders," I reply. "Much, much lighter. Totally."

"Excellent," she replies.

As I sit there, I become aware that the space seems brighter.

The rays of sunlight are now filling the room. *How appropriate*, I think, feeling, myself, like sunlight on air.

Looking back now, I think that sometimes in life, we can get so low that we do not see our purpose, our reason for being here at all. But if we can find a reason, we can pick ourselves up and go on, we can *choose* to go on . . . on to endure that unhappiness, that inner agony. We may not find that level of happiness we are reaching for, but we find a level of being at which we can subsist for a while as we wait for our true purpose to show itself. And that is what I did.

My children, my girls became my purpose for many years and that was a *fine* purpose, a *fine* reason to sacrifice, to endure my unfulfilling marriage, my disease, but maybe not for my *entire* life.

How much do you live for other people? Yes, life is about giving, but what about when the giving becomes an endless sacrificing of yourself? How much do you sacrifice what you *need* to make you happy? And if you have to forsake your happiness for a time or for others, then for how long do you do it? How long before the great, deep unhappiness of your soul grinds your mind and body to dust, drains you of energy and the will to go on? Even the happiness one experiences with her children is no substitute for the energy that comes from a love for your own life.

In order to answer these questions, I know I must first go back and answer a more primary question. How did I learn to do this as a habit, to set myself aside, squeezing myself out to make room for what *others* wanted or demanded?

Maybe if I answer *this* question, I'll begin to understand where this self-negating drive came from. Then I can begin to unlearn it. I can begin, instead, to learn how to live *my* life . . . my one precious life.

1

A TELLING DIAGNOSIS

My story begins some time ago. Yet the scene returns to my mind—the memory precise, each emotion so close it seems as though I can touch it, as it permeates the very fiber of my being.

I am there now . . . on that day . . .

It is 11:00 in the morning and I feel as if I've fallen into a void. The year is 1987. I am 38 years old. I feel no fear. I feel no sadness. I feel no peace. I feel only an emptiness beyond imagination. Where am I in this vacant space that now exists within me? I know only that I am *here*. Or, at least, the shell of me is here.

Step by step, I continue down the wooded country road I have so often walked.

The massive pines stand erect like sentinels, guarding whoever passes beneath them. Their branches stretch outward as if they are holding up all of the unknown wants and desires of humankind. What about my desires? Are they holding mine up, too? Do they even know what they are?

"Are you listening?" I whisper, "I'll tell you. I want to feel whole, complete, filled. I want to know true love." But those desires are not to be.

The dirt road falls away beneath my feet. The gray sky hovers as if in wait for some cosmic event.

Or am I feeling this because of the devastating event that has happened to me?

As I continue to walk, I try to recall the path that has brought me to this day, these challenging circumstances. I was the person who set out with such positive aspirations and dreams for my life.

But now, the emptiness pulls at me like fingers gripping at life's tenuous threads of my heart. I feel myself plunging down . . . down . . . down.

The birds *must* be singing, that melodious blend of perfect pitch sound, but I do not hear them.

Are they my chickadee friends who seem to follow me wherever I go or are they the incredible nuthatches that hop up and down the trunks of the trees I have such a fondness for? I do not know, for their sounds do not reach me.

The wind *must* be blowing, giving me the sensation of lift, yet I do not feel its strength. Is it a gentle breeze that greets me or the forceful gale that announces a coming storm? I do not know, for my senses are dulled.

The roadside flowers *must* be blooming, the scene awash with the blend of their hues, yet I do not see them. Are they my favorite wild daisies or are there some buttercups popping up? I do not know, for my senses seem nonexistent.

The questions keep galloping through my mind. *When* did all this happen? *How* did all this happen?

Why did all this happen?

I have always found Nature to be my best friend and companion, offering wisdom and insights that would have been impossible for me to receive in other ways. Yet, now I feel myself adrift, lost in a sea of emptiness, silent and alone, vacant, dulled by my recent news.

My thoughts begin to wander back, trying to understand how I, the one who always tried so hard to do the right thing, could have wound up in this place where life seemed to be turning against me. Where had I gone wrong?

I had moved to this small town in the northern part of the Adirondack Mountains of New York State seventeen years earlier. Here, I'd been greeted by very friendly people as I wandered down the main street. I, myself, had been born in a small town some ninety miles away at the western edge of the Adirondack Park. Small towns were my preference, and I was excited to find an opening here upon graduating from college.

The interview for my first teaching position had gone well. Days later, they had offered me a job. This is where I would make my home.

I married the following year, and we purchased some property. I marveled at the view we had of Algonquin Mountain in the far distance.

I did not realize then that Algonquin stood as a noble representative of the 46 High Peaks which would become a vital healing tool for me in the future. We moved into a home on our land and took up residence there.

We struggled in our young marriage, both of us having come from homes where there was little evidence of healthy communication or mutual support. I even question whether there was any semblance of true love. We were both consciously ignorant of that at the time.

I want to be clear that I am telling *my* story and no one else's. My husband and I were two entirely different people, though we didn't realize it at the time. Like so many couples, we were not emotionally suited to each other. We were the wrong puzzle pieces, trying over and over again to fit together.

We each had different needs, different expectations; even our roles became mixed. I guess you could say that we adopted our families' examples of poor communication.

Insecurity reigned, allowing power and control to become a dominant, destructive presence in our relationship. Where were the love, understanding and compassion that I so sorely needed? I began to question whether true love lived there at all. Then, again, what was I expecting? How was I defining true love?

As time passed, I could no longer recognize my husband. We had become friends before marrying and enjoyed each other's company. Maybe, though, we had not become *best* friends.

I had taken my wedding vows to heart and tried to become appealing to him. Somehow I had come up short. It seemed to me that he now came to ignore me when he was at home, rarely sharing any feelings except anger and frustration.

His criticisms of me became more and more frequent. He seemed irritated by my questions and even my laughter. I found that he began substituting television, thick novels and use of the computer for the sharing and communication I so yearned for.

After supper my husband would sometimes teeter at the top of the stairs like he was an inmate awaiting his release. Then he would proceed to the basement where his relief was housed, either in his office or in the family room. His office was home to the computer he had become affixed to, and the family room housed the television and the thick novels for which he had acquired a passion. I felt like mistresses had entered our marriage, stealing his time and attention away from me.

Though our intimacy was rare, I had birthed two beautiful daughters who were quickly becoming my lifeline, as sure as I realized that they could not save me forever.

My husband was an attentive father, wrestling with the girls when they were little and even changing their diapers when they were babes. He would at times read stories to them, and often got up with them when they had scary dreams in the night. I hoped that they would look back on their childhood as being happy. That was my wish and I tried to insure that memory.

I had begun to feel like an empty vessel waiting to be filled . . . just waiting. Is that when the profound sense of emptiness really began? I'd done a superb job of ignoring it until now.

I continue down the road past an opening in the trees where I had, years earlier, taken my daughters to play in the leaves. A smile tickles at the edges of my lips as I remember watching them scamper about in the piles with such delight on their faces, such delight in my heart at the sight.

The stand of hardwoods surrounding the opening is now bright, the summer foliage fully open to the sun.

This fall, these trees would drop their colorful leaves, with them cascading down like snowflakes adrift on the wind. Would we again make piles to jump in? Maybe. I remember a poem I once wrote, the words flooding back to my mind—

The leaves descend like falling rain
Upon the covered ground,
Falling gently, twirling some
With hardly any sound.

The wind gives lift to random ones
As up they climb on high.
But just as quickly do they fall,
And with the others lie.

All dried and scattered are they now
As autumn closes down.
And winter snows will settle them
With seldom any sound.

And with the warmth and sun of spring
The snows will melt away.
The leaves will dry and fertilize
The ground on which they lay.

And nourishment will they provide
For grass and moss and fern.
Nature's cycle thus complete,
From Death does Life return.

Will I recover from this dying that I feel inside? Can I weather this winter of my life, and one day feel the snows melt away?

Have faith, I think. *Have faith that one day my life will return.*

I realize that my senses are returning as my memories pour forth, positive and negative. Balance is the important thing. But, can I maintain a balance? I feel my life tipping more and more to the negative as I feel weighed down by the burdens I carry.

As I come to a bend in the road, I pick up a stone in my shoe, a minor burden for sure. Yet, the further I walk, the more painful it becomes. It reminds me of life itself.

If I don't remove the stone, the pain will become unbearable. How often have I left the stone there, absorbed the pain and carried on? I have a tendency to ignore clues along the way until something happens that forces me to sit up and take notice. That's what is happening to me now.

But what am I supposed to notice?

I allow my mind to drift back to earlier days, the days when I first became aware that things just weren't right within my body.

Months before, I began noticing physical sensations that were not normal for me. Day by day, my left hand was becoming more and more difficult to close, despite my efforts to concentrate. I began to worry. It was like a connection was broken between my brain and the muscles in my left hand.

The hand was scary. It was getting weaker, less coordinated. I worried about it more and more, and found it hard to concentrate on the things I needed to do.

Only the girls could take my mind off my dilemma, and I

gave them my full focus. I could step into their world in a moment and spend hours there.

Very soon, I noticed that my left arm felt exceedingly tired when I went to raise it, as if it was being pulled to the earth by imaginary strings. It felt so heavy. At that point, I had not experienced any physical pain but I had noticed that the right side of my back felt like it wasn't even there. No matter how much I tried to rest and give my arms a break, too, I felt exhausted.

As the symptoms piled on, I was in a quandary as to what was wrong.

Of course I feel tired, I told myself. *That's just my normal state. I think I've actually been tired for years.*

Despite the troubling symptoms and exhaustion, I still performed my household duties and, of course, was a mother to my girls. They were my priority.

In addition, I had taken on, in the last few years, part-time work in my daughters' elementary school, providing them and the other children with a quality physical education program. I was fortunate that it was not a full-time position, though energetically it sometimes seemed as though it were.

I ran after school tumbling and gymnastics programs and organized demonstrations for the parents. I held after school Modern Dance classes and choreographed Creative Dance assemblies. I loved working with the children. Besides, I wanted to keep my hand in my profession for the day that I would return to the full-time work force.

I decided to save most of the money I was earning for a few trips for the family: Boston—site of Revolutionary War beginnings, the Smithsonian, and finally Disneyworld. And I did it!

We made all three trips! I really knew how to save.

What was it really costing me besides the money? I was skimping on any time for my own personal relaxation. There was always work that needed to be done. Besides that, I only bought clothes for myself which were necessary and on sale. It had become easy to talk myself out of buying almost anything for myself. But for someone else, if I had the money, it was fun!

And I never rewarded myself with a purchase or a treat. Guess I felt that I didn't qualify. I hadn't *earned* it. I wasn't good enough. Ah, yes, I was the queen of sacrifice . . .

I was trying to be the perfect wife, the perfect mother and the perfect teacher. *How had I gotten that way? Did never doing well enough in my parents' eyes have anything to do with that? Could I ever be satisfied with ME?* I wondered.

I persisted in being what my husband wanted me to be, or as I *perceived* he wanted me to be. I spent time cleaning, cooking, mothering and budgeting. You see, even though I had a part-time job, the budget didn't change. I just had money now to save for our trips. And save I did!

By nature, I was a curious person, always asking questions. My husband would get frustrated by my questions. He did not want to discuss feelings either, neither mine nor his. So, our conversation dwindled.

I wanted more energy, could have used more energy, but I was *okay,* chalking up my tiredness to how busy I was.

Things progressed slowly, becoming worse day by day, month by month . . . until one morning my hand wouldn't close at all. I was shocked. My left hand hung limp at my side like a cooked spaghetti noodle hanging off the end of a fork. Each day I had hoped to see an improvement. There was none.

Inwardly, the fear was building. I tried to maintain my bright cheery façade. I didn't want to worry the girls, trouble my husband or be a bother to anyone, so I kept doing all my tasks as before, one-handed.

Upon awakening one Saturday morning, I quickly got up to get breakfast going. *What would I make today?* My girls were waking up and I could hear them talking in their bedroom beside ours. My mind was racing. *We'll have the English muffins I made yesterday and maybe some scrambled eggs or I could make tofu waffles. They're a favorite but they take longer. And I didn't plan ahead for this morning. So it's going to be scrambled eggs.*

After cooking and serving and cleaning up from breakfast, I made sure the girls were dressed, hair combed and teeth brushed. My husband was off to play golf so the day was ours and I had set my cleaning goal for the day.

I would wash the walls in our bedroom today—all four of them. My sister had told me that she washes all of her walls each spring. Well, it was past spring and I'd never washed mine at all . . . EVER! So, today was the day.

While the girls busied themselves with playing dress-up and creating plays, I began my task. Pouring warm water in the pail with some detergent, I began wiping down one wall at a time. It was difficult to move furniture with one hand, but I was strong for my five foot, one hundred and five pound stature. Besides, I had taught physical education and had kept myself in good physical shape even after having the girls. So, I managed.

First I would wash the wall, then I would rinse it, and then I would wipe it dry. I decided to start by doing one wall completely. This task involved climbing up and down the step stool to reach the higher areas.

After washing one wall, I was beat. I collapsed on the bed, knowing I still had to rinse and dry that first wall. I felt the energy leaving me like the tide rolling out to sea, leaving the shore far behind. *I'll recover in a bit. I just need a break.*

I awoke to the sound of two excited little girls rushing into the bedroom where I had fallen asleep. They were staring at me, looking startled.

"Oh. I guess I dozed off," I said, sounding groggy.

As I sat up and looked at them, I began to chuckle. They were dressed in costumes which they had created without any theme in mind. They were a conglomeration of style and color, complete with wigs and high heels that were a bit too big for them. They had scarves wrapped everywhere around them. I was always amazed at what they chose to put together.

"You two look great! Here, look in the mirror. Have you seen how you look?" I asked with an admiring tone in my voice.

They grinned with glee, posing and twirling and flipping those scarves all around—so innocent and excited. They turned and chased each other out of the room to work on creating a play in which they would have the starring roles.

So, now that I was fully awake, I got up to rinse my wall which had already dried with the soap bubbles adhering to it. The next thing I knew, however, I heard the voices.

"Mommy! Mommy! Will you watch our play?" the girls

called.

"Of course," I yelled back.

I climbed down from the step stool. At least I'd gotten the higher areas rinsed. The rest could wait until after lunch.

Lunch. I'd almost forgotten what time it had gotten to be. Okay, first the play and then the food. They sang two songs and then acted out some dialogue, my older girl giving her younger sister cues when she forgot her lines.

Play over, now they were hungry.

I decided to have some of the homemade chicken soup that I had made yesterday, the broth coming from the chicken bones that I had cooked up. Then there were leftover waffles.

"Mommy, could we have waffle sandwiches with peanut butter and some of that green stuff?" they asked.

"You mean the bean sprouts on top?"

"Yes. They make my teeth shudder when I eat them," said my oldest daughter.

"And I like the sound they make when I bite into them," her sister replied.

"Then waffle sandwiches it will be, after some soup," I said.

I was glad they liked the nutritious food I tried to prepare for them. It took a lot of time but I didn't mind. I got the unsweetened peanut butter from the food co-op I'd joined in our town. The tofu waffles were made with whole wheat flour and a number of eggs. It was their favorite. I felt satisfied with the menu.

"After lunch, Mom, can we play a game outside? Like hide and seek?" my oldest asked.

"I don't see why not," I replied.

So after lunch we found ourselves outside, hiding our eyes and sneaking around to discover where each was hidden. I laughed, the girls squealing at each discovery until I felt the tide going out again and knew I had to quit.

I went inside and lay down on our couch, not able to face the rest of the unrinsed wall in our bedroom. After a while, I got up and went in to finish rinsing the wall to get rid of any streaks and call it a day . . . almost.

My husband arrived home from his golf game and decided he was up for having a late lunch. He really wasn't into our tofu, bean sprout and waffle sandwiches, preferring the waffles hot off the griddle instead. So I made him a BLT.

After feeding him lunch and cleaning up from all our lunches, I went back into the bedroom to lie down for a while. The smallest task seemed to tire me so. I began to doze lightly until I was jolted awake a few minutes later by a chopping sound outside our bedroom window.

My husband had decided that it was time to chop some wood. Being such a light sleeper, I felt every explosive delivery of the ax as a sledgehammer bludgeoning my skull. I got up, saying nothing to him, for fear that his anger would erupt. I could never tell when or why he would explode. His anger reminded me of my dad's, though he wasn't as loud, and would send chills through me every time.

He was not physically abusive to any of us but would, at times, disappear into the woods where, if I listened closely, I could hear him cry out his frustration, inner anguish and agony with a loud piercing yell that nailed the very marrow of my bones. I somehow felt that *I* was the source of his frustration, yet I didn't know what I had done to cause it.

It was easier to keep quiet, to avoid the confrontation; easier not to ask him to stop chopping, easier to just go without a nap. And so I did. I didn't want the girls to grow up with all the constant tension that I had experienced, so if I could prevent that, I would.

I hadn't gotten to the laundry today and it *was* wash day. I proceeded to collect the dirty clothes, sort them and load the washer. With that done, I remembered that the fourth of July was quickly approaching.

I always enjoyed decorating the house. Maybe that was an outlet for my creative side. This occasion called for red, white and blue accents. Since my brother was a Korean War Veteran, I decorated in honor of him and all who had fought over the years to insure our freedom. I felt very indebted to them all, and I wanted to instill that sense of patriotism in my daughters, too.

So we began to create, making paper flags and hearts. They were taped everywhere with few restrictions. I draped fabric remnants, which I had kept from clothes I had made for the girls, with just this purpose in mind. Accents in place, I realized it was time for supper.

Maybe I'll just serve spaghetti tonight and a green salad. I have some sauce I made last week in the freezer. I just have to cook up some beef for the sauce. I should be able to do more, but I'm really very tired today.

After supper was prepared and served, and I had put away the extra food, my girls came running into the kitchen where I was standing.

"Mommy, can we go for a walk? Please?" asked my youngest.

"Does your sister want to do that, too?"

"Oh, yes. Yes, she does," she nodded vigorously.

"Okay," I said. "Ask Dad, too."

It was not uncommon for us to take a walk after supper. Dad usually joined us. It was a family outing. Sometimes we would stop and visit a neighbor who had younger children and they would all play together while the adults visited. It was a positive social time for me and I usually enjoyed it immensely.

This time, however, I felt like a wrung out dish rag, my physical energies totally depleted. Yet, from somewhere, my emotional energies kicked in and carried me through as I saw the delight on their faces.

"We'll do a short walk tonight," I announced. "Mommy's kind of tired." Actually, I was exhausted and feeling quite badly that we couldn't take a longer walk this evening.

"Okay, Mom," they replied, disappointment showing on their faces.

After the walk and the bedtime routine, with them all tucked in, I'd tell them a story which I'd create on the spot. Usually, the woodland characters that I chose would experience the same challenges that the girls had during that specific day, this time with a peaceful ending.

"Goodnight. Sleep tight. Sweet dreams," I'd always say.

Then, I'd crash.

I finally realized that I couldn't bake all the bread I used to, or keep up with all the housework. Fortunately, school was no longer in session so that part of my life was on hold for a few more months.

It was very difficult for me to ask for help, even opening a jar. It made me feel as if I were a failure, a state I had felt so often in my adolescent years. It was a sunken feeling, like being in a deep cavern with no way to escape.

There were so many things I thought I needed to do and I never got to the end of my list. Eventually, I could not drive myself anymore. I was worn out. I finally admitted to myself that this could not go on. I had to get answers.

I had been seeing my family practitioner ever since my first daughter was born ten years earlier. I liked him. He was personal and competent. He never made me feel like he was in a rush, and gave me his total presence when I was there. I guess he made me feel important for those thirty minutes of my appointment, and that was very special to me.

As I sat in the waiting room, I began to notice that my left leg felt like it was resting on ice cubes instead of the cloth covered chair I was sitting on. *How can that be?* I wondered. *Cloth doesn't feel that cold and my other leg doesn't feel that way.* The sensation was noted but dismissed.

After checking things out, the doctor presented the possibility of carpal tunnel syndrome for my wrist. I went away thinking that if that were so, an operation could remedy my problem. He recommended I see a neurologist and his office called to make the appointment.

As the in-between weeks passed, I began to experience pain in my left wrist. The sharp piercing sensation would streak like lightning up to my shoulder, catching me unaware. At other times, the pain would be dull for a spell. I was always surprised by what it would do.

There were now some numb feelings extending to my diaphragm and over to my stomach, like tentacles of numbness reaching and stretching all over my body. At times, it seemed I was short of breath. *Maybe that's because,* I finally admitted, *I'm scared now, really scared.*

Finally, it was time for my final reevaluation. I was back again in my doctor's office, this time to hear the conclusion which both the neurologist and he had reached. As I was settling myself in a chair in the examination room, I noticed my doctor wasn't smiling as usual. His eyes seemed to have lost their sparkle and his face looked very serious. He then spoke, gently and kindly.

"The neurologist feels, and I agree, that you have Multiple Sclerosis."

It took a second for the words to register. Then the numbness that had been spreading through my physical body became a growing numbness that spread through my mind . . . my heart. Just like that, I had been diagnosed with a debilitating disease. I heard little else he had to say.

I remember asking him, "Can I still ride my bicycle?" I had been riding six to ten miles each day on my old three-speed for exercise.

"Yes," he answered, "just don't exhaust yourself." *Exhaust yourself,* I thought, *that's my usual state.*

After hearing his instructions, my thoughts immediately flashed to the girls. What would become of them? Of me?

I left the office and traveled home, stunned, feeling like something was squeezing me inside. My physician had said to call him anytime with questions. That had given me a good feeling, but not quite good enough to overcome the shock of the news.

As I began the ride home, I gradually, and surprisingly, became aware of a peacefulness creeping in even as the tears streamed down my face. I didn't experience doubt or denial. I didn't experience the heat of anger. There was a knowing within me.

This diagnosis had to happen.

Where had that thought come from? I shook it off and focused on the mundane world of all my duties. How was I to live with this? How would I function?

While I believed the diagnosis, I did not altogether understand this disease in whose grip I found myself. It was like a prison of non-performing nerves, caging the high performance person I was trying so hard to be.

The woman who could perform and never stop.

The woman who had no personal needs at all.

2

AN UNSPOKEN REVELATION

continue my walk down the country road, my heart still and dulled by the insights that flood my mind. I realize I am allowing only my mind to act right now, as if something is blocking all feeling within me. *Maybe I'm in shock,* I think, trying to understand what is happening to me and why it's happening. *Maybe I'm not supposed to know . . .*

As I come to the next bend in the road, I stop suddenly, frozen in place. Anguish racks my heart as tears gush from my eyes and run in torrents down my cheeks. The dam has finally broken!

"God, how could you have allowed this to happen to me? I've tried to be good my entire life, doing things for other people, helping them on their journeys. Why? Why this? Why now? What do You want from me?" I ask searchingly. I am sobbing now and the pain is extremely deep. I feel like a hole is being torn in the fiber of my being.

"I'm not going to believe in You anymore. No, I'm not. That's it!" I half-shout, half-sob.

I take a deep breath as my emotions quiet and my tears subside. Slowly, I feel myself taking on a stoic demeanor, a cloak coming down on my feelings once more. I realize that I am denying that God exists, that *my* God exists. I feel that He has betrayed me.

I turn away. I have never felt like this before . . . so alone . . . so hollow . . . so void of any substance at all. I am but a shell of the person I was.

I become aware of the atmosphere around me. There is only stillness—no bird calls, no air movement, no wildflower aromas... just stillness, like the whole world has stopped moving . . . *my* world. And it has.

I begin to turn around at this bend in the road. As I do, I find myself beginning to smile and a chuckle escapes my lips. *Imagine that*, I say to myself. *Here I am, trying to deny God and, yet, I'm speaking to Him. Not much denial there.*

"Well, I guess we're in this together then," I say aloud. "Please give me the strength to endure whatever may lie ahead."

With that, I continue down the road back toward the house, still smiling to myself. Again, I begin to feel the breeze as it moves across my face and catch the aroma of the wild flowers along the roadside. I now can hear the chickadees chirping out their familiar song.

As I move, I become aware of the *way* I am moving, almost sauntering as I return home. I feel a sensation of peace . . . for a while. I no longer feel that God has betrayed me, but I don't understand why this is all happening to me—why He is allowing this to happen to me. What good can come out of this? I see only pain and struggle ahead. *And hasn't that been what most of my married life has been so far? Except for the special times with my*

girls, it seems like I've lived with this emotional pain forever . . .
even before, way before.

I feel that there are secrets, happenings that are locked away
in my subconscious, even in my cells—things from my past that
are affecting me now. I push this idea aside and allow my mind
to drift back to my return home after being given my diagnosis—a
scene ingrained in my heart for all eternity.

When I arrived back at our house in the woods, I sat staring
at the structure surrounded by flowers.

I opened the car door as our dog, Nobbin, bounded up to
greet me, her tail wagging furiously. For a split second, the emptiness felt the touch, the presence, of something wonderful—a
bright energy.

How nice it was to be greeted with such unconditional love.

Slowly, I walked over to my husband who was working outside. He turned and looked my way with interest. As I reached
him I said, "The doctor says I have Multiple Sclerosis."

His face went blank. He turned and walked away saying,
"We'll get a second opinion."

"No!" I called after him. "I believe it!"

And that was that. No hugging. No holding. No comforting.

What was more telling was that I was not surprised. Once
again I'd been hopeful, although this same man could not even
cry with me when I had miscarried our third child the previous
summer. I had nearly begged him to share my tears. Maybe he
was unable to, that not being a part of his makeup.

Tom had become quite unaffectionate with me over the past
fifteen years. From the beginning, I became aware that he didn't

have much desire for the hugging, holding and intimacy that I had assumed would be such an integral part of our marriage. Could I accept that? I knew now, for sure, that I *hadn't* accepted it. I couldn't. I wouldn't. I needed that show of affection to validate my own sense of worthiness, especially now after this diagnosis, not only as a wife but as a person.

Our marriage felt empty. *I* felt empty.

I had kept trying to change the person that I was, thinking that if I could become what he wanted, whatever that was, our relationship would improve and he would become more affectionately demonstrative toward me. Nothing I had tried so far had worked for me. So where was I? Standing there on the lawn, I felt as I had for so many years—truly alone. Void. Unloved.

I have so often felt unloved in my life, I thought as I walked on. *Not by my girls, but by everyone else. Where has that feeling come from, and why does it feel ingrained in my very cells? When did this pain and sense of being unloved and unwanted begin?* These roots seemed to be deep, like old themes, in my life.

Another question crystalized in my mind, a question which seemed to point the way to what I needed to know. What was it like—the home and family I was born into? That's where *my* story actually begins. From what I'd heard and otherwise pieced together over the years since then . . .

It was a frigid day in November, 1948. The snows had come early that winter, the ice crystals dressing the trees with shimmering icicles that glistened in the winter sun's reflection.

Rose and Stephen Havas made their way along the ice-covered roads at 4:30 in the afternoon as the sun was dropping.

Their destination was a hospital in the North Country town of Lowville, New York, eight miles away.

Rose tensed with each contraction, praying that they would arrive there in time to deliver her fifth child, the fourth having been lost in miscarriage the previous year. As the next contraction came, she told herself, as if the telling would make it so, *We have to make it in time . . . we have to . . .*

As her eyes lifted to the window, she saw the trees begin to bend. *The wind must be picking up,* she thought. The sun became cloaked in white as a mass of gray cloud began moving across in front of her. The gray became darker . . . and darker . . . and darker until it seemed as if the sun had disappeared totally.

They were immersed in a darkness so complete it was as if she were in a cave deep within the bowels of the earth. The car lights shone through a thick fog of snow so dense that the light reflected back in upon them.

"What is it?" Rose cried. "What's happening?" The fear and near panic in her voice was evident.

"What do you think it is?" shouted Stephen. "It's a blizzard! Great timing on *your* part!" he added accusingly.

Stephen slowed the car to a crawl, hunching his body over the steering wheel, his nose within inches of the windshield. Rose closed her eyes and tried to calm herself. Her mind leaped back into her past, to the account she'd been told of her own birth.

I remember my mother telling me, Rose began thinking back, *that she had named me Rosalia, after her favorite flower. How special was that? She told me once that roses had a smell that was "Heaven's scent". How* appropriate, *for their smell is certainly heavenly. Someday I'm going to have a garden full of roses and I'll pick one each week to have on my dresser and I'll think of my mother.* Rose inhaled deeply and sighed at the memory.

She and her three siblings had crossed the mighty Atlantic Ocean in 1908, immigrating from Hungary to America, the land of opportunity. Her mom had carried Rosalia as a babe in arms to meet her father for the first time. He had traveled months before, and, having found work, had sent for his family to make the crossing.

After their arduous journey, their ship was detained at Ellis Island, actually placed under quarantine, for smallpox had been diagnosed onboard. To her mother, the only thing that made the wait bearable was the sight of "Lady Liberty" which brought a tear to her eye each time she gazed at the massive symbol of freedom, freedom she so longed to feel as she raised her family in this new country.

As they awaited the vaccine's arrival, Rosalia's naturally curly auburn-colored hair was, as required, "shorn off like the wool from a sheep, leaving her bald and barren" as her mother had described it many times over the years. It had never grown back as curly, but it was a small price to pay since they had all avoided contracting that dread disease.

As Rosalia grew, her hair shone with subtle red highlights framing her face. Her mother, Anna, referred to her as her "blue-eyed rose" and so 'Rose' she came to be called.

As the car continued to creep along in the blinding blanket of snow, Rose took a deep breath. She had to do something to keep her mind occupied between contractions and away from Stephen's mounting irritation with her as well.

Her Catholic schooling left Rose enamored with the nuns, so much so that she dreamed of one day entering the convent. Her mother disallowed the notion and the dream was shed. Still, she kept her religion close to her heart for her entire life.

After high school, she had fallen in love with a shoe salesman. Her mother forbade the idea of even dating him, stipulating that he wasn't Hungarian, so that was that. Rose often wondered how much better her life might have been if she'd been allowed to date him. Would they have eventually married? Well, she'd never had the chance to find out. *I wish Stephen could love me like I need. "Loving" is so mechanical with him. I want to be held and appreciated,* she thought.

The next contraction was beginning as Rose gripped the door handle and held her breath. *"Please let us get there in time,"* she pleaded silently to God, as she squeezed her closed eyes even tighter, every muscle in her body screaming for relief.

With its passing, she looked over at her husband, his ice white fingers gripping the wheel as tightly and constricting as the grip of her contractions. His position hadn't wavered. The snows had not relented. They crept along in a veil of whiteness, only the headlights illuminating a semblance of direction. Rose began to relax once again and breathe more deeply. Maybe recalling her reaction to Steve the first time she saw him would shift her focus for a while, to a time of youth and promise.

We met at a dance, Stephen being the drummer in the band. He seemed so worldly and had such dreams . . . Oh, how handsome he was, five feet ten with raven black hair and chocolate brown eyes. I was only five feet tall and ninety-five pounds at the time, a real peanut next to him.

When he asked me to dance, I thought I'd melted right there. That broad body enveloped me in his arms and I was lost, swept off my feet, as he guided me around the dance floor. How he could waltz . . . There wasn't a dance Stephen didn't know.

He was confident and capable. He'd learned many skills out there in the world. I didn't care that he had quit school after eighth grade. Even so, he always sent some of the money he earned home to his mother who was still raising two other boys.

And he was so smart. Any girl would have found him quite a catch. Yet he chose me! We courted and he proposed.

Then I learned that another had returned his diamond ring to him and now it was on MY finger. Well, such is life.

Stephen and Rose married on November 16, 1930. Two years later she bore Lenora and a year after that along came Stephen, Jr., who came to be called Buddy. *He was such a buddy to me,* she recalled as a smile crept across her face.

With the Great Depression in full swing, followed by World War II, at least they'd had an income as Steve worked long, hard hours at the shipyard. Those years were all a blur. Their frequent moving, five moves in ten years, did not encourage long, deep friendships to form for any of the Havas family. There were no good-byes to be said to anyone.

When they moved to Hoboken, New Jersey, Rose recalled, it

was to such a tiny residence that it required Stephen to leave his beloved drum set behind. *I think he left a part of himself behind. His drums and his love of music both seemed to disappear that day and Stephen began to change.*

With the birth of their third child, Bonita, Rose realized she had nursed all three of her children. What a great start in life she had been able to offer all three.

With the war winding down, Stephen moved the family, for the last time, to the rural and desolate area of the North Country in upstate New York. Actually, they were eight miles out of the town of Lowville on a back country road at the edge of the Adirondack Park. There, on a fifty-four acre parcel of land which would one day become *my* respite and refuge, Stephen hoped to fulfill his dream of becoming a chicken farmer. Rose looked forward with hope for a new life. Yet, neither was going to happen.

They took up residence in a carriage house which had been built on the property. The children began to refer to it as "the chicken coop". It was TINY. It had no running water and no indoor *necessity* as it was called back then. The only heat was from the wood stove which also served as the cooking station.

Bud and Lenora became the water haulers, lugging the pails which were filled from a creek one hundred yards away. They were eleven and twelve at the time. Of course they could endure it for a spell, but the spell had now been four years . . . four years! Drinking water, bathing water, washing water, cooking water . . . summer and winter . . . for a family of five!

I was exhausted. We were exhausted, remembered Rose. *Bonita was only two when we moved there.* Rose began to feel those stirrings of regret swell within her. *How was she going to bring another babe into this? How?*

Another contraction began as Rose's hand tightened around the door handle, trying to prepare herself for the knife-like pain she would surely encounter. She had been through this three other times.

My miscarriage had been the worst. I'd been hanging the washed clothes outside on the line when it occurred.

Steve didn't hold me or comfort me. It was like nothing had happened. He went to work as usual and told Buddy to stay home from school to care for me.

I wasn't allowed to grieve out loud. I held my tears inside of me, in a secret room known only to me. There I was free to mourn my babe, the life that was a part of me. A little part of me died with that babe and never returned. It must have been my fault. Somehow I was to blame and now I'm being punished. I say my rosary each night for that babe, that babe in limbo.

"Steve, where are we?" she dared to ask, her voice quivering with anxiety and fear as she stood on the precipice of tears.

"How much further? Are we going to make it in time?"

"Shut up! Just shut up!" he yelled back at her.

Rose shrank back against the door, clinging to the handle for a very different reason this time. A lone tear slowly crept down her face. *How had Stephen gotten this way?* She wondered. *He had become so hateful . . . so bitter.*

After Stephen moved them to rural, isolated Lowville, New York, he had used up all of their savings to live on, even cashing in the children's life insurance policies which were for their education. *All of this happened because his PRIDE wouldn't let him work for what he considered too low wages here in the North Country—big man of the world. Right. That stubborn Hungarian pride,* thought Rose.

So, here they were now with nothing, nothing at all. His dream of becoming a chicken farmer was not working out, either. *No house, no dream, no money. What will become of us?* Rose began to feel panic creeping into her very bones. She had to dispel this fear.

"Steve, Steve, I can't!" screamed Rose as a contraction squeezed her abdomen mercilessly. Tears burst from her eyes, soaking her cheeks and the front of her coat.

"Hold on!" he yelled back at her, fury in his voice.

My God, my God, what have I done to deserve this? she cried, awash in her own self-incrimination.

At that moment, Stephen turned into the hospital driveway, tires spinning, and slowly progressed up to the front door, stalling there. He threw open his door and rushed around the car, plowing his way through the newly fallen snow. He opened Rose's door and extended his arm as she grabbed on and lifted herself.

Step by step, they made their way to the door where the nurses were waiting. The contractions were quieting as they helped Rose inside. It was as if the babe knew they were safely here. Stephen bade her good-bye and left. She was on her own . . . on her own again.

At 8:34 a.m., on November 21, 1948, Deborah Diane, weighing eight pounds, inhaled her first breath of air in her new world. She acknowledged her entrance with a full-bodied shriek which startled and surprised both doctor and nurses attending the delivery. Rose, who was sedated throughout the procedure, awoke to view her new little bundle with raven black hair that stuck straight out all over her head like the bristles on a brush.

This babe would not be breast-fed like her siblings had been. Rose was too worn out; so worn out from the life she led, in fact, that the doctor insisted she remain in the hospital for two additional entire weeks.

Maybe she was even too worn out to show her love to this little one who had been placed in her care.

The day came for the trip home. Rose, a bit more rested but still fatigued from her delivery at age forty, prepared herself for whatever awaited her there. Wondering how the children had fared in her absence, the ride home with Stephen was quiet except for the baby's gurgles and cries as she experienced the bitter cold air for the first time.

Turning into the snow-covered driveway, it was evident that Buddy and Lenora had spent many long hours shoveling. Two feet of snow had fallen since Rose had left, leaving the banks that edged the driveway with the appearance of mountains lining the way.

After parking the car, Stephen helped Rose to exit. Suddenly, a shriek erupted as the bitter cold wind struck the baby's soft pink skin. Rose pressed the child to her as she hurried to the front door.

As she entered, Rose's gaze swept the room. The wood stove faced her against the far wall. The wringer washer stood against the wall on the left with the wash tub on the floor nearby. The cooking utensils and food were set on wooden shelves aligned along the left wall, along with the doorway to their bedroom. The table sat in the center with the chairs gathered about it. There were no couches or comfortable chairs. *Maybe someday,* thought Rose.

On the right she saw Buddy, fifteen, hovering in his doorway, anxious and fearful. Beatings by his father had taken their toll. Lenora, sixteen, entered from the girls' room, also on the right, where she had evidently been playing with Bonita. She walked over and gently gave her mom a kiss.

"It's good to have you home, Mom," she whispered to her. Then she reached her arms out for the baby so Rose could remove her coat and hang it on her empty wooden peg by the door. "Is this Deborah?" she asked as she gathered the pink bundle in her arms. "Hi, little one," she said as she unwrapped her new sister.

Bonita had moved over to where Rose was taking off her coat, wrapping her arms tightly around her mother's legs. Rose patted the top of her daughter's head as she plopped down in the nearest chair to remove her galoshes. Bonita turned and glared at her new sister, resentment beginning to build at the attention she was already stealing from her.

"What's for lunch?" demanded Stephen. "Let's eat."

"I'll get right to it," answered Rose anxiously, as she struggled to rise out of her chair. Things hadn't changed much since she left. Life had not escaped her. It was ever present.

That was Rose's welcome home. And that was also Deborah's. There wasn't any excitement to be had, just apprehension and dread. Often at night, Deborah's cries could be heard with the resulting response from her father.

"Shut up!" Stephen would shout, awakening Lenora who would then arise to collect her new sister, change her and feed her the bottle before putting her back down to sleep. Rose was too tired to even get up.

Looking back, I realize that I came into this world at an inappropriate time in an inappropriate place. I was a mere inconvenience to all. Mom had neither *been* allowed nor had *she* allowed herself to grieve her previous miscarriage. There was neither time nor energy to do so. How was she, therefore, to bond with this new little one?

My presence meant another mouth to feed, another drain on the monies which were already absent, another child vying for Mom's attention, another voice piercing the night with cries, another amount of laundry, another requirement for water to be hauled. I cried much of the time, feeling unappreciated and stressed.

Mom didn't have much time to hold me and she didn't have the energy to produce enough breast milk to feed me. My desire to be held and comforted and cuddled by her was high. I wanted and needed *her* love to help relieve the tension I sensed all around me. Always on the verge of tears, my muscles would tense and squeeze tightly, my heart beginning to quicken. And when I cried, the tears would pour out in desperation as if in emptying myself of them, the tension around me would cease.

But it didn't. It was endless and I was *helpless* to affect it.

The tension would envelope me, closing in on me, attacking me—threatening to overtake me at any moment. I couldn't escape it. It was everywhere, a strained and terrifying introduction to this world, *my* world.

I know that my sister Lenora, then sixteen years old, did her best to comfort me but she wasn't Mom. For two more years Lenora continued to give me her attention until she was sent away. Still, I needed *Mom's* time and attention. The lack of it resulted in a craving for something I couldn't reach or replace. It produced in me a deep absence. I didn't feel of value to anyone, not even myself.

This absence transitioned to a belief that I was unworthy somehow. It was that void that would evidence itself through my growing years and well into adulthood. It would form the weak basis on which my self-image would take shape, clawing at itself as if precariously hanging from a ledge. Would it abruptly drop out of sight or climb out of the waiting abyss?

I wavered between those two choices, year after year. No matter what I accomplished or how hard I worked, I didn't feel that it was good enough, that *I* was good enough. I needed to do it all as perfectly as I could imagine. I became driven, but driven to what? At the time, I didn't know.

That was the past and this is the present. It helps explain quite a bit to me—my intense need to be held and a basic feeling of insecurity. *But can I change any of it? And how will it affect me in the future?*

I wonder.

When I was a babe, my "home" did not feel safe to me, neither the structure nor the people in it. My husband's reaction in turning away from me at such crucial times as the miscarriage and my diagnosis also makes my adult "home" feel unsafe. *Will I ever find a safe "home"? Maybe . . . someday.*

Walking past a row of Norway spruce, so majestic in their stand as they hug this road I love to walk, I'm struck with a new thought.

Maybe it was the image I created of my husband that I used to fill the emptiness. Maybe I so badly craved affection that I projected onto him. I just knew it was there, and that if I said or did the right thing, it would pour out for me, for ME.

Now, as I proceed down the road feeling this void again, I gasp. Another thought strikes me. I was the one who chose this marriage, this marriage where the emotion I so craved was all but nonexistent.

I had said yes to him, even though he had shown me little affection from the start. At the time, I was relieved, being so inexperienced with boys. Having become friends, he had been the first one to ask me to marry him so I thought I was supposed to say 'yes'.

My dad had not allowed me to date in high school. In college, I began to avoid boys, becoming uncomfortable around them with the way they looked at me. I had married a man who didn't look at me that same way.

My dad had shown me little, if any, affection that I recall. Is that one reason I craved affection so? Was I expecting this man to fill the void my dad never had?

I know that I need to forgive my dad, but not now. I'm just not ready . . . yet.

3

IN LIMBO

A few days later, I found myself kneeling at my bedroom window. *What's happening to me?* I wondered. *Here I am at thirty-eight years of age, but where* am *I exactly?* I looked out at Nature—the trees, the cloudy sky, the colors. My husband hadn't spoken to me about my diagnosis in three days. *Why can't he hold me and comfort me?* I wondered longingly. I felt a deep ache inside me, like I was breaking slowly in two.

All of a sudden a force came plunging into my awareness and I realized—*I am all alone.* The depth of that aloneness was so absolute. It encompassed my whole being. *I feel void . . . vacant . . . nothingness.*

Where does this feeling come from? How did I get here? I keep pretending all is right when so very much is wrong.

I crumpled to the floor in utter desolation. My tears gushed as my body was wracked by soul deep sobs. After a time, my sobs quieted. I had no doubt at all that my husband would do his best to pay any and all of my medical bills. But I also saw now that he *would* never, *could* never be *there* for me, emotionally and psychologically, in my need. *What am I to do?* The thought plagued me.

I lifted my head slowly and stared at my hand. The sun had emerged from behind a cloud, its brilliant rays streaming in through my bedroom window. I saw reds and blues, dancing on my fingers like a prism of color—*bullets of light . . . bullets of hope.*

I lifted my body and looked around.

"I am within the sun's rays," I said aloud as my flow of tears subsided.

I could feel the warmth, being in the sun's radiant light. My spirits lifted and I knew that I could go on, I *must* go on.

Taking a deep breath, I whispered, "Give me the strength to endure."

I felt as if I were on the outside looking in at normal people living their lives, going and doing with all their might. *Hadn't I been going and doing the same as they were?*

As I sat up, I thought, *But what about just* being? *I don't know how to just be.*

My whole identity seemed to be bound up in doing for others. It was only then that I had any feelings of self-worth. *But I can't do for others right now. So where am I? Who am I?*

My thoughts took the form of a poem:

Energy, how dare you!
Haven't I done right by you?
Haven't I used you to help all others?
Ah, yes, but what about me?

As the day progressed, my girls demonstrated the normal ventures of childhood, and I grew as much as they through it all.

They were eight and ten at the time. The *real* challenges began then, not as much with them as within myself.

My first challenge struck me head on. *"How do I tell my girls without creating panic?"* Thinking from their perspective, they only knew that I went to see the doctor because my hand was limp. They didn't ask me how the appointment went when I got home. That bought me some time to think about this hurdle.

Oftentimes it's the parent's panic that precipitates the child's reaction so I had remained calm on the outside while inside, I quaked and quivered. *I'll do it, I'll tell them . . . when I feel the time is right.*

I decided to simply state the truth since there was no sugar-coating this diagnosis. I reminded myself that how I relayed the information would affect how they received it and reacted to it, how they processed it.

Unfortunately, our neighbor at the time also had MS and had progressed to a wheelchair. The girls and I often visited the horses that lived on her farm. We picked and fed them the grasses that grew under the fence, surrounding their field. I worried that my girls would picture *me* the same way and become scared, but . . . maybe not.

I knew that they could not possibly imagine, at *their* ages, what it was like for someone to be told she had a chronic illness. How I *did* the telling was the trick—my tone, my body language, my demeanor. If I didn't communicate panic, they probably wouldn't feel that way either.

Hours passed . . . the time arrived. *Here it goes.*

"Girls," I called as they came running down the hall. "Come sit on the couch with me. There's something I want to tell you."

Strangely enough, I wasn't nervous. They plopped down next to me. I looked at their smiling faces and I wondered what they had been up to.

"What were you two doing?" I asked.

"Just playing, Mommy," one daughter replied while her barefoot sister sat and played with her toes.

The innocence of children is so wonderful. That may help get me through.

"So, you know that I went to the doctor a few days ago about my hand, the one that isn't working well." As I said this, I raised my left hand and let it dangle in the air for a minute. "Well, he told me he thinks he knows what the problem is." They continued to watch me, eyes glued to my face. "The doctor feels that I have Multiple Sclerosis, but that doesn't mean that I'll end up like our neighbor, Jennifer. It does mean that I'll have to take more naps and I'll need you to be good helpers."

"Okay, Mommy, we can do that," said my oldest, matter-of-factly. Her sister shook her head in agreement.

"Can we go back and play now?" asked the youngest.

"Of course. Have fun. I'll be in to check on you soon."

The girls jumped up off the couch and tore back down the hall. *Mission accomplished.*

Neither one cried. Neither one panicked. I had stated my diagnosis as a fact of life, our life for now. And we all continued on. My first challenge had passed.

My next challenge was telling other members of my immediate family. My brother and two sisters expressed surprise and caring. They were all living a distance away with their respective families. They each told me they'd keep in touch and I was sure they would. But I didn't see their faces or feel their hugs, the hugs I sorely needed right then.

Shortly after *that* hurdle was over, I needed to tell my principal and a few close friends. It was important to me whom I told, and in what order. Was that because I needed to have a bit of control in this uncontrollable situation that I found myself in?

I invited my principal and his wife over for supper. After we'd eaten and visited, I shared my news.

"Oh, Debby," his wife said as she rose from her chair and approached me with her arms open wide for a sincere hug. Tears cascaded down her face. I cried, too, and we shared a special moment, one I would never forget. It felt so good to me. My principal remained seated, a look of shock written over his face.

"I request a leave of absence for this school year," I said, holding my breath.

"You have it," he replied.

I could feel the relief sweep through me. I knew that my body would need time to begin to heal if that was the route it would take, and I would need time to adjust to whatever my future would be.

I firmly believe that the body always tries to heal itself. *We* are the ones who must find the ways to support it so it can begin that process. And that's a tall order, for sure.

Information from the MS Society arrived and I delved into it, wanting to know everything I could about this frightening disease.

Tim, the director of the Albany chapter of the MS Society, seemed to be quite committed in his mission. On the phone he greeted me with understanding and compassion. He listened, supported, explained and recommended. He was really knowledgeable about the disease that was plaguing my body. And he knew about the research and what it was saying. I asked him question after question. He didn't seem to tire or become impatient with me and I appreciated that. My spirit felt lifted, at least for a short time.

I believe that knowledge helps to combat fear. If I can understand what is happening in my body, maybe I can figure out how best to support it.

After I scoured the materials, I piled them on my husband's dresser.

He didn't seem to have any interest. They sat there untouched day after day after day. He asked me no questions about my illness.

How is it possible he has no interest in knowing what's wrong with me or the pain I'm in?

As I started to tell my friends, I discovered that many of them already knew of my diagnosis. That infuriated me. I felt cheated at not being able to tell *my* story, *my* way, the *first* time.

The thing was, I needed support right then and I wondered what they'd been told. It was similar to grieving. People have to tell the tragedy over and over again to get through it, to be able to move on. I needed that, too. I needed to see the surprise on their faces, feel their hugs, share some tears. I felt that the opportunity had been stolen from me. No one had asked my permission. I needed to be able to control *something*.

I was realizing that I couldn't stand being talked about. During my childhood, my family was quite secretive about what went on inside the home, where we went and what we did, but we knew people talked about *us*. Now I was feeling that sense of violation.

People were talking. Why was no one calling to express concern?

My next challenge was to go grocery shopping. I had been dreading that task, but it couldn't wait another day. What would happen when I came face to face with people? I had been teaching in this town, on and off, for seventeen years. I didn't know everybody but many knew me. How would they react? Did they know? It concerned me a great deal.

I felt embarrassed that such a thing as this disease could have happened to me, as if I could have prevented it somehow. Did the voice inside my head come from my religious education classes of long ago where God was presented, not as a merciful and loving Creator, but as a punishing Father? Is that why I was having a difficult time now relating to this Creator?

The fact was, I'd begun to question my faith again and was doubting. I was experiencing a very uncomfortable feeling deep inside, a clutching, closing down kind of feeling. I didn't like it. It wasn't a good feeling at all.

Put those thoughts and feelings aside. Right now I need to go grocery shopping, I told myself.

I drove down the black-topped road and arrived safely at the store. As I proceeded down the first aisle, I got a surprise. It was my close friend, Sally, turning down the same aisle and coming towards me. It was so good to see her. *I wonder if she has heard.* She glanced my way, but before I could even smile, she turned around and reversed direction, going back around the corner.

I could feel my heart sinking. *She turned away, my* friend *turned away from me.* I couldn't believe it. I tried to choke back the tears but they began to tumble out anyway. I wanted to shout at the top of my lungs, "Wait! I don't have leprosy! You can't catch it!"

I so needed to feel acceptance right then, especially from my closer friends. My gaze traveled to the floor as my heart plummeted to the very depths of my being. After a few moments, I dared to look up a little, fearing sight of anyone else I might know. I took a deep breath and quickly finished my shopping, focusing only on the products lining the shelves and on my list of necessary groceries.

As I checked out, I didn't even make eye contact with the clerk, much less speak to her. I gathered my bags and moved out the door. Proceeding to my car, I settled my bags inside and climbed in.

I was in oblivion as I drove home. I had no knowledge of even turning onto our road. It was like I was on automatic pilot, in escape mode. All the while I was feeling like an outcast in society—no longer a participant at all. The scar began to form, running deeper than I could ever have imagined.

The days became weeks and the weeks became months. Trying to carry on a *normal* life required going out into public and so I continued that task, cringing every time. Many times after that initial shopping trip, I experienced what I came to refer to as my *leprosy moments* as I saw people avoiding me, turning away from me or no longer including me in their lives. These were people I had previously thought of as my friends. *Where are they now?* I thought. These moments were just that, *moments.* Yet, they had a dramatic effect as each exposure served to peck away at an already low sense of self-worth.

While I felt many friends turn away, two acquaintances came forward. My relationship with each of them gradually became a special friendship, a major source of support for me.

Why did they both bother to initiate contact with me? I wondered. They invited me to their homes at *my* convenience, since they had become aware that I needed to take naps each afternoon.

I realized that most people are actively involved in their lives during the afternoon hours. That eliminated me right off the bat. I felt guilty that I needed to sleep so much while others were out going and doing. At the time, I didn't realize that this was my body's way of slowing me down so it could try to heal itself. And there was a lot to heal.

Yet, these two women somehow understood. They seemed to accept me and what I was going through. It meant the world to me.

Our conversation revolved around normal things, positive things, aspects of life and living. I needed that normalcy in my life, something to balance my everyday experience. Their friendships provided me with that.

I sometimes asked myself, *Haven't I earned the right to be free of disease? I've exercised routinely, done all my own healthy cooking, and always put others needs before my own. I go to church regularly and have even been told that my smile cheers others on their pathways in life.*

But deep inside, there was a vacant place known only to

me, which reared its head now and then, when I felt the need to defend myself, when I felt threatened. Often my reaction was held within, deep within.

I raised the questions aloud, "Why me? Why this? Why now?"

But those passed quickly through my mind as if I was not to contemplate their answers at this present moment. Maybe I was not *ready* to hear the answers yet.

I gave voice to the core question for me, "What am I supposed to learn from all this?"

Through my experiences, I had found that people who made a habit of finding fault with others were very insecure themselves. Finding fault placed them at a higher station *above* the other persons, or so they believed. It was a power play to protect their own senses of worth.

When others referred to my 'poor health', they were not acknowledging the fact that I was still able to ride my bicycle and climb mountains. They preferred to concentrate on my inadequacies, as they chose to see it.

Oftentimes I heard comments like, "But you look so good!"

Was I supposed to be wan and fragile looking? Was I supposed to be lying in a bed all day? What were they thinking?

It was a gift and a cross to be looking normal while diagnosed with this disease. It made me realize that I often conjured up expectations from the way a person looked. If I were to look wan and fragile, others would not expect much from me. Looking good created an expectation of normal activity and behavior, even when fatigue descended, a catch-22 for the diagnosed.

I am able to move
But I don't.
I want to move,
But I can't.

Fatigue is a state unseen, unrecognized by the general population of humankind. It is as unseen as the undertow at the raging springtime waterfalls. Yet, it is as inhibiting as anything can be.

Everyone understands being tired. Few understand the numbing, crippling wash called fatigue that I experienced each day. It did not continue the *entire* day. I didn't know when it would arrive or how long its visit would last. These ups and downs of desiring something as fleeting as having the energy to physically answer the phone had, indeed, another side to them. What about having the energy to carry on the conversation? I'd never had to consider that before.

Now I had to ask myself if both energies were present. Sometimes they were and sometimes they were not.

I heard the phone ringing. *Do I answer this time*? I asked myself. There was a lot to consider before I made my decision.

Today I decided, *No, not right now.*

I knew that I was able to pick up the phone, but I was unable to be *present* to the caller. *That* required energy.

There was some self-recrimination that began to enter. How could I be present to others when I did not even have the energy to be present to myself? This line of thinking was nothing short of devastating and drained me in and of itself. I gave this state of fatigue a name. I called it 'my zombie state'.

I was there physically, and, yet, not present to anything or anyone. I did not even seem to care anymore. Caring required energy. I then came to understand, a bit, how some people could reach a point where they considered taking their own lives. Yet, even that required energy. I wondered if they were in similar states, though the causes that brought them to this point might be different. I realized even thinking any thought at all required energy. That energy, I did not then possess.

Energy, where are you?
How elusive you are.
I would see myself desiring you,
If I had the energy.

I did not *want* to do anything. I did not *want* to be anywhere. I did not *want* to be anyone. It was the *wanting* that takes the energy, I realized.

Much of my life I had spent trying to be someone I was not, trying to fit another's image of who or what I should be. People had tried to mold me into what *they* wanted and I allowed it, thinking so very little of myself. I never felt that I had met their expectations. I rarely *felt* successful even though I had succeeded, earning both a Bachelor's Degree and a Master's Degree, even having conducted research for my thesis. I had taught in both public and parochial schools, full-time and part-time.

I had developed curricula and conducted hands-on creative programs, strongly believing that all children could learn that way successfully. Not all students were successful with the strictly academic/worksheet method so prevalent in the schools at that time. By anyone's measure, I had been successful.

Anyone's but my own.

I had run a household through careful budgeting. Even so, when monies were not adequate I would creatively scrimp, making my own greeting cards to send out and rationing postage stamps. Nutrition and exercise were my emphasis, cooking from scratch and growing a garden so we could have fresh vegetables.

I had begun substituting raw honey and molasses for refined sugar in recipes and halving the sweetener, whatever I used. I received much criticism from both friends and family for these practices. The fact that I had different beliefs was pointed out to me with a negative tone of voice by any who thought to express it.

Around me I saw others, whom I admired, doing things differently from me. They seemed to run normal households. I was threatened by that and by them. Therefore, I believed that I really *was* different and maybe even *wrong. They must be correct*, I thought. It never entered my mind then that maybe, just maybe, *I* was the one who, by doing things differently, was a little ahead of my time, and that one day, the future would dictate a more conscious adherence to a holistic way of life.

I had sought to provide the best possible home for my two daughters. I would tell them each day that I loved them. I found something to compliment them about each day, also noting a special quality they had or reinforcing a positive behavior they had exhibited. I felt I had not experienced that in *my* growing years.

As time went on I became aware that my identity was bound up in the *doing*, which, of course, required energy. The cooking, cleaning, exercising, teaching and raising children all required energy.

I realized that it also took energy to be pleasant to others whom I encountered on the street. Even asking the clerk in the store about her children required energy.

It took energy to be positive and energy to be negative. Either stand attracted more of the same. When I was happy, I seemed to attract other happy people. Through sharing the happiness, it seemed to grow.

Contrarily, when I felt down, others who were down seemed to find their way to me. Consequently, I plummeted further.

I had to be selective as to which phone calls I answered based on whether I had the energy to be present to the caller. I also had to consider where my positive or negative level of energy was at that moment. Was the caller going to lift me up or pull me down? I didn't need any more *negative* energy.

Then there was the conversation to be considered. Listening took energy even more than hearing the words. And last of all, I needed to interpret them. All of this required my deliberation each time the phone rang.

Furthermore, as time went on, I found that it took energy to distinguish one object from another, one person from another or one thought from another. It took energy to release forgiveness to those who had hurt me in the past. I knew who was at the top of my list but I could not imagine forgiving *him* at that time. Maybe someday.

So, what was I to learn from all of this? Having energy had been such a focus for me all of my life. That was what I had become—a transmitter-like vessel of positive energy. My achievements were in areas requiring physical abilities and, therefore, also requiring energy. Sleep had become extremely important. If I didn't get much, I wouldn't have much energy and, consequently, my sense of worth was lowered. My bounce, my smile required positive energy. So, now, what if I didn't have any? Was I being called to a deeper awareness of who I really was, my true identity? Is that why I'd been allowed this time of not moving very well? Was that a clue?

As with most things that I became aware of, I knew this would be a gradual journey. But forgiving my dad? THAT would require energy—energy that I just didn't have right then.

It was kind of interesting how people got into routines no matter what state they were in, healthy or otherwise. And so my *morning* routine had taken on an added twist in addition to combing my hair and washing my face.

Each day I would awaken and find myself going through a body check, sometimes even before my eyelids caught the light. I began at my feet. *Can I curl my toes?* I asked myself. *Tightly or with just a bit of movement?*

Next I would ask myself, *Are any toes lying there like dead wood?* If so, sometimes I could concentrate really hard and make them move. Other times, I didn't have the energy or desire to even try.

Does my big toe feel all numb and frigid inside even though I can move it? I asked myself. I found that if that part of me felt numb, I could call it into action if I visualized that part moving inside my head, the mind-body connection being very strong indeed.

Then I moved my evaluation upward to my knees, thighs

and hips. *All okay?* I asked myself as I climbed upward.

Upon reaching my chest, I checked in further. There was a band of numbness across my solar plexus where sometimes feeling was nonexistent. The band seemed to change in length and/or width and intensity daily. It was a dull absence of presence inside although if you were to touch the area, I could still feel your touch. I didn't understand it at all.

Sometimes my back hurt, the pain traveling up and down my spine like race cars zipping around the track, and sometimes it felt like a tortoise making his way home.

At times, my heart ached. It was a descending, sinking feeling, like a stone dropping to the bottom of a pond. I was so shocked by this sensation that I began to fear my heart stopping completely. I wondered if it was possible for this disease to have that effect.

I began to think about my nerves carrying messages from my brain to my muscles. I knew that the lessening of myelin which covers and insulates the nerves could prevent the efficient transmission of impulse. Since the heart was a muscle, I asked my doctor about the possibility of my heart stopping.

"Your heart stopping would not occur because of the Multiple Sclerosis," he assured me. I was relieved.

Is my left hand moving a little better today? I asked myself as I continued my self-examination. At times it was and at times it wasn't. It could change throughout the day. I never knew. I couldn't plan. It was a hope-filled action which I attempted each day. Consequently, some days I began with very little hope.

I found that when I focused on a negative thought or feeling, like an ache or a pain, the resulting limitations engulfed me like a shroud, pressing me down into the depths, fathoms deep. I was amazed at the strength of the intensity of each emotion I experienced.

Each day I had to decide where my focus would be. If it was on a negative symptom that I was experiencing, I was inhibited in my activity level for the day. So, I wouldn't take that walk in the woods that I loved. Visiting my friend to cheer her would have to wait for another day, and there would be no baking a cake that I so enjoyed.

Instead, I tried to focus on a more positive approach. I learned to take my walk and try to accept that it needed to be quite modified that day. I felt that movement helped to heal the body as long as I didn't *exhaust* myself, as my doctor had cautioned me.

I would visit my friend for a *short* time to cheer her, leaving my personal baggage at home. Bringing the focus to *her* would give me a much needed break from my own problems. I'd pick a flower from my garden to take to her. Cheering someone *else* always gave *me* a lift, too.

The cake would have to wait until tomorrow. *But who am I disappointing?* I asked myself. The answer was obvious, *only me because it was one of my goals for today.* Pertaining to goals, I realized it was better to have only one goal each day for now. Then, if I was able to do more, that would be a positive thing. If I had many goals and didn't or couldn't accomplish all of them, it would seem to me that I had failed. I learned to clean my house at a rate of one room each day. *There I am again, emphasizing the doing. At least I realize it this time. That's a first step.*

I realized it was all about learning to read my body. It would let me know how much I could do on a given day if I not only heard it but really listened to it. And it might tell me not to *do* anything, just *be*, for a change. Could I be comfortable with that? Would I be ridden with guilt? I knew it would take time.

It's all in the expectations, I said to myself. Was I *expecting* to do something or *hoping* that I could do it? Hoping was a much more positive approach and didn't set me up for failure.

I looked forward to tomorrow and the cake I *hoped* to bake. That was tomorrow. That was a beginning—a *new* beginning for me.

4

SURROGATE SCENARIO

At times, the daily fear I lived with seemed insurmountable, gripping me inwardly like a fist clenched with each breath I took. I feared a flare-up of this disease.

Every twinge, every numbing sensation I experienced could be the beginning signs of yet another deterioration of the myelin, the insulation coating my nerves. Or it could be a normal constriction of blood flow to that area of the body. It was hard to tell.

There was no one who I could share my fears with. I felt loneliness invade my world daily, covering me like a shroud. Yet, I went onward, sometimes pushing it aside, sometimes burying it beneath daily tasks. Sometimes I would succumb to its power and let the tears flow, feeling the fear tear at the very fiber of my being. But up I would come, again and again and again. I never felt completely rid of it.

Friends who had distanced themselves around the time of my diagnosis remained at a distance, and I still did not know why. The two new women who befriended me grew closer as time passed. Maybe I scared the others away. Was it because if this diagnosis could happen to me, what might be in store for them? I was not one to gossip or complain about my private life so what else could have driven them away? I couldn't imagine it was anything I'd knowingly done.

I found it interesting to see who could maintain a friendship with me afterward and who backed away. I didn't think that I, as a person, had changed at all. But maybe I had.

I began to become aware that I might have an ulterior subconscious motive. At times, when I surprised someone with a flower, a visit, or a jar of jam, I asked myself if I was doing it to cheer *them* or was my neediness directing the action, like a red flag waving in the breeze saying, "Don't forget about me. I need you to notice me and support me now."? Was I trying to *buy* their friendship so they would think of *me*? Or were my thoughts along this avenue only a result of my trying to deal with my diagnosis?

I decided to stop second-guessing myself and focus on a positive, unselfish motive. I did enjoy surprising and cheering up people I knew. Doing so cheered me up, too.

I fought the feeling of being victimized. I was *not* my disease, even *if* others looked at me that way. I came to understand that my body had a dis-ease and I wanted to give it support, healing support.

Why was it that I wasn't merely disappointed when friends turned away, but I actually felt *traumatized*? There was an intensity about it. I so needed the evidence of caring, the show of love that I wasn't getting at *home*.

Once upon a time I *had* felt the support, the encouragement, the acceptance and the love. I did have that for a spell. Somehow, the memory of a time past, when I'd felt unconditionally supported, kept coming back to me, and I found myself going back to a feeling I longed for now.

When I entered junior high, I would arrive at school each morning, my school bus unloading at the side entrance. After I passed through the door, I would proceed straight to the girls' locker room.

The locker room was laid out with many rows of gym lockers, each row facing another row with a long bench in between. The gym lockers themselves were small since the gym suits that we were required to wear took up little space, but there were taller lockers for hanging up the clothes that we were changing out of. The lockers were gray metal, the benches a light natural wood of sorts. There was a shower room, also, with dual showers and private changing areas for use after swimming and gym classes.

Once in the locker room, I would place my books on the nearest wooden bench and search my coat pocket for my comb with my one destination in mind—a mirror. The mirrors were located at the end of each row of lockers. Each day, right off the bus, that is where I would head and position myself. There I could comb my hair and get out all the tangles before anyone else could see me. And there was another reason.

I went there each morning because I had a strong desire to make contact with one person—my gym teacher. Her office was in the center of the row of lockers. If she was there, I could talk with her. It was like getting my dose of emotional support for the day and all would be well. If she wasn't, well, maybe I would see her at lunchtime or at another time during the day. We didn't even have to make eye contact. Just *seeing* her was a boost.

For various reasons, my gym teacher was quickly becoming my favorite person. Yes, I was worried that I wouldn't perform well in front of my classmates, but little comments she made to me caused me to suspect that she thought I had some athletic abilities.

I wondered if she actually liked me as a person. I didn't understand, at the time, how starved for affirmation I really was. What was it about her that affected me so?

For one thing, she always seemed relaxed and approachable. With her short brown hair and sparkling brown eyes, she immediately put me at ease. I welcomed her into my world. Her smile warmed me and her eyes seemed to throw sparks when she laughed. She would sometimes wink at me as I struggled to learn the skills or moves that we were working on in class, moves like the prone-to-prone headstand, and that spoke volumes. *You're doing fine. I'm glad you're here.* That was the message I always got.

While she was gentle in spirit, she also had a strength of her own. There was self-confidence in her demeanor, yet she was kind. As time went on, my admiration for her grew, as it did for another person who was taking an important place in my life.

My brother, Bud, was fifteen years older than me. He'd been my idol ever since I could remember. He was my five-foot ten-inch hero with a medium muscular build. As a child, I was intrigued with the big wave that he would comb into his brown hair right in the front of his head. It meant the world to me that, when he wasn't at work, he gave me time and attention. It told me 'You are important'.

When we were together, I experienced a deep, warm glow that filled me and radiated out to my extremities. I tingled with excitement and happiness when I was with him. My time with my brother gave me a sense of wholeness, a sense of feeling good about who I was, even more so than the positive feeling that arose from my gym teacher's affirmations.

Given that I often felt unstable with the shifting moods at home, my brother always being there for me brought the balance and stability that I so desperately needed. He began to influence me in ways neither of us was aware of at the time.

For one thing, he loved the out-of-doors and had wanted to become a forest ranger. Since that education cost money, and there wasn't any, he enlisted in the Air Force for four years. When he returned, I became his tagalong helper when he went out to the woods to hike around. I loved that! We found peace and quiet there, and did little talking.

We harvested seeds right from the cones and planted trees. He would make a slit in the ground and I would insert the seedling. Then, with the heel of his boot, he would stamp a few times to force the air out so the roots wouldn't die.

I learned a lot about the different kinds of trees and what the various woods could be used for. For instance, cedar could be used to line closets and hope chests where people stored clothes. Red pines, with their tall, straight trunks, when mature, were used for the masts of ships. He was an encyclopedia of information about Nature.

Weekends, too, we often went to the local drive-in movie theatre together. Bud would get behind the wheel of his four-door, sky blue Rambler with a stick shift. I would open the door to the front and place myself inside, adjusting the seat much closer to the dash than it usually was. Once there, I would be overcome with a feeling of calm as if I were escaping from something and was, at last, free. We talked and laughed all the way. One time we rode home with no headlights, because the wiring was malfunctioning. My brother drove slower that night, but I was never afraid that we would crash. I was in good hands, I knew. It was amazing how well I could see after a while, even in the pitch dark.

We even crept through an abandoned cemetery one night, just for the scary thrill of it, Bud shining his flashlight on the eroded grave sites and the leaning tombstones. It was spooky, yet I experienced a kind of sadness at the lives that had come and gone. Some had been children, others had been mere infants. Some were of the same family, and some had even served as soldiers of past wars. There they all were, lying together . . . still . . . silent.

It was obvious that some grave sites had been forgotten. A few had plastic flowers on them still, faded by the onslaught of snow and rain and years of disregard. I wondered when they would be replaced, if ever.

It was hard to read most of the tombstones, but I came away with appreciation for life and its finality. The eroded graves had caved in and when we shone the light on them, I'd almost expected to see parts of a skeleton lying there. We didn't see anything like that, of course, but the main thing was, I was doing something that would terrify many children, and doing it without fear—all because my brother was there.

The forest became my playground. We had fifty-four acres of land and I roamed much of it. Along the way, I took to climbing trees.

What a delight it was when I reached the tippy top of a tree. I could look out at the world, *my* world. When the wind blew, I could feel the trunk sway and I was forever the eagle soaring in the sky . . . gentle, consistent, calm, peaceful. It was a cloud-nine experience for me and I loved the feeling that was so high, so free! My sister, however, called me a tomboy because of it, over and over again.

When I became a cheerleader as a sophomore in high school, the most wonderful thing happened. My brother began dating my phys. ed. teacher. I was ecstatic. Miss Smith, Bud and I would ride home together in the same car after the basketball games.

I had quite a curious mind but never felt comfortable asking questions in my classes, afraid of what my classmates might think. In the car with them, I could ask away without reserve. There was no fear of reprisal, no fear of being laughed at.

We would all get into the car and settle in. We'd make our way out of town, turning on to the country road which led to our house, eight miles away. Then I'd begin my questions, whatever was on my mind.

I knew that my brother had spent a lot of time in the woods, and I assumed that Miss Smith knew something about Nature, also. Given that she was a phys. ed. teacher, I supposed she liked to be outside, too.

"I was wondering," I began, "do all weasels turn white in the winter, like rabbits do?"

"No," my brother answered, "some keep their natural brown color all year round."

"Are there two different types then?" I asked.

"There are many types," Bud explained. "It's the short-tailed weasel that turns white. The longer tailed weasels keep their natural brown color all year round."

"So, are the white ones albino then?"

"Animals that we call albino stay white all the time, not just in the winter," Miss Smith interjected. "And albinos usually have red eyes, I believe."

"That's right," Bud confirmed.

I was still curious. "Is there a special name for weasels when they turn white?"

"Ermine," both my brother and Miss Smith answered at the same time.

We all laughed, and Bud continued to explain. "The short-tailed weasel and the ermine are just two different names for the same animal, which has white fur in winter here in the northeast. Out on the Pacific coast, the short-tailed weasel stays brown all year round."

"You probably know what I'm going to ask next," I continued, feeling sheepish. My desire to know was warring against my embarrassment that maybe I should *already* know the answer.

"What's the summer stage called?" they both responded as they glanced at each other and winked, proof that they were thinking the same thought.

We all laughed again, a bit harder this time. It was so great to sense that these two people whom I loved so much were that in sync.

"I think it's called a stoat," Bud answered. "But don't quote me on that."

"Those are really good questions, Deb," Miss Smith commented. "Hold onto that curious mind of yours. That's a really good ally to have."

Later in life, that comment would return to bolster me during a time of much more serious questioning and seeking.

Times like this made me feel so good. I felt that they both thought I was intelligent and had a good mind. My questions never seemed to bother them and they always responded to me. If they knew the answers to my questions, they would share them with me. If they didn't, they'd attempt to problem solve an answer or admit they didn't know.

I experienced a oneness made up of all three of us. We were a unit and it made me feel stronger inside, temporarily. I was accepted, supported, respected and loved. What more could I ask for? I looked forward to each occasion of being together with them, anticipating the good time we would have—another dose of emotional support to help me get through.

After we got to our house, we would all go inside and gather around the dining room table, joined by Mom and Dad. We'd share hot tea and cookies that Mom had baked. I was pretty quiet inside the house and merely listened to the conversation.

Too soon, the basketball season was over and those *family times* ended. I was saddened by that but there were still some occasions when we could travel together, albeit fewer. I knew that nothing could ever replicate those evening rides home, with me questioning, them answering and all of us laughing so hard, but I remained grateful for those special times. They had nourished my soul.

Cheerleading try-outs came again for junior year, and I worked as hard as ever. We were required to try out with a partner since synchronicity is important in cheerleading. It didn't matter how well I had done at the games. A group of people whom

Miss Smith had selected sat and judged us as we performed two cheers.

When I finished my cheers, I tried to read the judges' expressions, to see what they thought of me. But there was no sign, one way or the other, as to how they rated my performance. They all just tilted their heads down and seriously began filling out their judging sheets. I left on pins and needles.

A week later, at our Girls' Athletic Association year-end banquet, Miss Smith stood up to announce all the awards, and finally it was time for her to list the varsity cheerleading squad for the following year. I waited, stone still in my seat. I knew I had good skills as a cheerleader and a nice smile, so maybe? As she read off the names, I began to realize that my name wasn't on the list. Did I miss it? Had she skipped it?

Reality began to sink in. I hadn't made it. I was speechless. My chest felt tight, my breathing constricted. I had so looked forward to my cheerleading.

I had been counting on making it onto the varsity cheerleading squad. I was recognized as someone when I was a cheerleader. It made me feel important. And it was rare for someone who lived way out in Watson to become a cheerleader. I was the representative for our area. I was proud of that. I felt like I was letting down everyone who lived there, especially me.

I felt my spirit plunging. *Now who am I? No one.* was the message that came back from the pain within. *What am I worth? Nothing.* I knew I had very good skills as a cheerleader. But how good I was didn't seem to matter. I wasn't good enough.

Leaving the banquet, I drifted down the hallway to retrieve my coat which I'd left in the locker room. I felt numb, in a daze, not present in this world at all. I felt utterly hopeless, vacant.

Miss Smith gave me a ride home. As we weaved along the country roads, I just stared out the side car window and didn't talk, not even a word. My mind was racing with negative head talk. *What makes you think you're good enough? You're NOT good enough. Yes, you thought you were pretty good. It was that pride, wasn't it? Squelch that pride! Look where it got you. I hope you've learned something.* And, indeed, I had.

I had dared to be proud of my abilities. *Never again!* Having Miss Smith in the car with me helped me to see what it's like when another shares some of your pain. I'd never experienced that before. I knew she was sharing some of mine but she couldn't carry the burden. That was up to me and me alone.

"I'm sorry you didn't make it, Deb," she said, sadness evident in her voice. "I tried to tell you to find another partner. I guess you weren't listening."

And I hadn't listened. I had ignored her suggestion. I had tried out with a new friend I'd made. She was a simple girl, and I'd hoped that she would make the squad, too. It was a mighty lesson for me.

Somehow beneath it all, though, a voice kept sounding. *You are not good enough.* When earthquakes occurred in my life, whether they were mere tremors or they rocked the Richter Scale, the message would boil out like molten lava, wiping out any gains I'd made in self-confidence or self-acceptance.

So, I was not a cheerleader my junior year. It was a tough year to muddle through. I spoke often with Miss Smith who cautioned me against developing an inferiority complex. She gave me a copy of the Serenity Prayer. Coming from her, it carried an additional specialness besides the wisdom of the words. *Accept the things I cannot change. Courage to change the things I can. Wisdom to know the difference.*

When the tryouts for senior year came, I decided to try out again. I had practiced and persisted. I was ready. I worked hard and this time I was careful in my selection of a partner. I gave it my best shot. And this time . . . I made it!

I knew I would take it even more seriously than before. Not having made the squad for my junior year showed me just how important it was to me, to my self-confidence, to my self-esteem. I needed to be a cheerleader. That was that. I planned to improve my skills and run efficient practices during my senior year. I'm not sure what would have happened if I hadn't made it again. But, fortunately, I didn't have to deal with that. My determination won out. I had worked hard and persisted. In my mind, I had, indeed, *captured the gold.*

At home, my oldest sister, her husband and family had come to visit. They would travel up from New Jersey where they lived to our house, a five or six hour trip. Traveling mainly in the evening, they would time it so their three little boys would fall asleep on the way.

When they arrived, they would whisk the boys into Mom and Dad's bedroom and tuck them in without any fuss or bother. The children were sound sleepers. They took over that bedroom because it was the largest and there were five of them. Mom and Dad were relegated to sleeping on the couch, but at least they wouldn't be awakened by little ones getting up in the night.

It was a rare visit and I loved it. She was sixteen years older than I was and would always bring bakery cupcakes, all decorated with colorful icings. My favorites were the yellow ones covered with chocolate icing and topped with sprinkles of every color imaginable. My mouth would start to water at the mere smell of them as she opened the box. We would all sit around the table, share the cupcakes and drink some tea, my dad having his coffee instead.

Then my sister would hand out little presents of food, or for me, when I was little, there was sometimes a doll. She was the person who bought me all of my dolls, and I loved every one of them. I pretended they were my students when I played school, something I did really often back then. I was older now and just enjoyed the camaraderie of us all being together. No one was upset or yelling. It was calm in the household and that was rare.

One day, while they were visiting, we were about to enjoy the dessert portion of our dinner. Mom had baked a chocolate cake topped with chocolate icing, her specialty and my favorite. As we began to feast, my brother-in-law turned to my brother with a rather serious look on his face.

"So, Natalie ended it?" he asked.

My brother sat there, staring into his plate, fixated on some tiny morsel remaining there.

I went into shock mode, frozen, stuck to my chair. *They're not dating anymore.*

My heart fell as if the ground beneath me was collapsing.

"No!" I shouted at him suddenly.

My poor brother looked stricken.

All I could feel was the foundation these two special people in my life had given me, and it was crumbling, minute by minute.

"It's all your fault!" I shouted at him.

Shoving back my chair, I fled from the dining room down the hallway into my bedroom. There, the dam broke and the tears flowed, soaking my pillow. I felt lost, in agony of spirit. *How can it be? The two people who supported me were no longer together. What would happen to me now?*

I had never been as happy as I had been when I was with them. They were the positive forces that got me through my days, weeks and months of feeling worthless. My wholeness was gone. I felt abandoned.

Somehow I knew that no one would understand my feelings, and now there was no one to talk with about them. I couldn't even talk to my gym teacher. I tried to carry on as usual, but my grieving was real and my heart carried the load.

Miss Smith seemed at peace when I next saw her. I continued my previous practice of stopping at the locker room where her office was. If the door was open, I would stop and share some of my life with her. She treated me as she always had, listening, commenting, encouraging my actions and interests.

When I explained to her one day that some of the boys in my class had approached me about sharing my homework with them, I told her my dilemma. I had spent hours doing the assignment, and I didn't feel that I should just hand it over when they hadn't put in any time doing it at all. On the other hand, I longed to be popular and maybe this would help. Her reaction was priceless.

"No way would I hand them my homework to copy. You did all the work, Debby," she exclaimed. "I don't think *friends* would ask you if they could copy your homework. They just want to use you."

I was glad that I had actually refused them their request. I knew that If Miss Smith agreed with me, then I was on the right track. I could respect my decision. The temptation was there though. *Would it make me popular if I shared? It wasn't worth it, if that's what it would cost.* I held tightly to that respect. I began to realize that was what I desired most—to be respected even more than to be liked.

Miss Smith's and my relationship continued until I graduated and even on through my college years. I wrote often, speaking of my dilemmas and soliciting her comments. I respected her views, weighing them carefully. And what was my major in college? Yes, it was physical education. She had written my recommendation and helped me practice for the physical tests that were required. I was anxious to be on my way.

After their breakup, I carried inside me the anger I felt toward my brother for quite a while. I knew it had to have been he who ended it, but I never asked and he never offered to talk about it with me. I had, in essence, lost one of the two most important people in my life, someone whom I felt I could count on to always be there for me, always listen to me, always accept the person I was. Those are the qualities a mother usually exudes to her daughter, but somehow I had missed out.

Undeniably, I was grieving my hopes and dreams of my brother and Miss Smith marrying. I felt shot down. Feelings just weren't talked about in our family. I avoided making eye contact with Bud or smiling much. Even though there was some contact with him, something had changed deep inside me.

I found it hard to get motivated, yet I continued on with my studies. Each day, the wall of anger that I was building grew higher and higher with more solidity in each block of concrete that I placed there. The more depressed I felt within, the taller the wall grew until I realized, one day, that I couldn't see out. I couldn't see outside myself. I couldn't see *my* world. I knew I had to do something, and I *could* do something.

I began to spend more time with my brother, doing things we had previously enjoyed doing together. I followed him out in Nature, collecting pinecones from the trees he selected and offering to help plant more trees. The anger began to peel away in layers like the layers of an onion and the solid base of love underneath became visible once more, week by week, month by month.

I never had any ill feelings toward Miss Smith about the breakup. I knew that it couldn't have been anything that she had done. How did I know that? In my mind, she was perfect, crooked nose and all. My contact with her had always given me positive feelings. I had felt accepted, encouraged, even loved. I knew my brother did have a few faults. I had heard him say things that weren't appropriate, negative comments about other races. So, it had to be *his* fault. It never entered my mind, at the time, that it could have been a mutual decision.

So, as I thought of college, I knew that I would write to her. She was still a special confidante on whom I could depend. I just wouldn't see her every day. What hurt the most, perhaps, was the fact that at first I had that beautiful emotional home base of acceptance, support and love that the two of them offered me together, and next thing I knew, I was watching it dissolve around me. First I had it, then it was gone.

Now that I felt a lack of support again, I realized that my brother and Miss Smith had become my surrogate parents during those years. Together they had shown me acceptance, encouragement, and even love which I did not, at the time, experience from my parents.

Back then, I had struggled to push aside the feeling which losing my "parents" had created. I had been given a bright gift—two people who liked me and showed me I had worth and importance. When that gift was pulled away, it left in me deep layers of hope denied and love taken . . . and the deep, deep pain of loss.

As I moved through my days now, I realized I still missed those times, and more importantly, the sense I had felt for such a short time that someone was *there* for me. That deep sense of loss and instability had never been fully erased. That "you are important to me" feeling which I experienced then had given me a sense of security in my young adult life. I now subtly sought more of the same. I was an empty vessel needing to be refilled.

But where could I go now to get my refill?

5

BUT AM I WORTHY?

My husband had become a deacon in our church. His course work involved me, also, two weekends each year, which afforded me the opportunity to become acquainted with Sister Catherine.

She eventually became my spiritual director and awakened my understanding of myself through the Myers-Briggs Personality Inventory. Her specialty area was psychology and counseling. Her position in the diocese required her to travel about, visiting each convent every month.

When she came to my town, we would meet. I reveled in her support of me. In a way, it supplied some of that parental emotional foundation I'd never had from my own parents and had lost when my brother and phys. ed. teacher broke up.

Along with Sister Catherine, Father Joe became a close and special friend. He was down-to-earth and real in every way, honest and forthright, kind and sensitive, a natural leader. As our family gathered around the supper table one evening at his rectory, he looked at me and spoke.

"Debby, I think you'd benefit from an eight-day silent retreat."

"Oh," I said. "Tell me more about it."

"The diocese is sponsoring one at Maria Renata on Lake Placid in July. I can get you the exact dates."

"Are you going?" I asked.

"Yes, I am. I went last year and had an awesome experience."

That settled it for me. I was ready to sign up. Interestingly enough, if Joe said I would benefit from it, I knew I would. I had no doubt. I had that much faith in the man. I was immediately intrigued by the idea.

This led to my driving down the sand and gravel road a few months later, on my way to a personal retreat. It was the summer of 1988. Trees hugged the shoulders of the mountain road, making me feel ensconced and protected. I was ready for this. I *needed* this.

I had only been away from the girls overnight once before, when I had my miscarriage two years prior. This time, I had written a note for each day I would be gone and asked my husband to tuck them under their pillows while they slept. Then they would find them the following mornings.

I had organized, cooked and baked all the meals and left a menu for each day. Besides, the girls could help, having spent much time with me in the kitchen. Their father had never exhibited an interest in cooking so that and all the grocery shopping had been left up to me.

I was uncertain of what to expect, never having been on a silent retreat before. Was I ready for what time alone might unearth?

My directions led me to a dirt driveway. As I turned in, I noticed columbine at the edge of the forest and then a few

Jack-in-the-pulpits nestled under the trees themselves. They looked very comfortable, standing there in the peace and quiet. Not too far off, painted trilliums swayed in the slight breeze.

On the opposite side of the road, a few blackberry bushes caught my attention. That reminded me of where I grew up and all the berries we used to pick. I welcomed the familiar feel of it all.

Reaching the end of the winding driveway, I parked my car and got out, looking at the woods surrounding me. The birds were whistling their tunes, and the bees were buzzing around the wild flowers that grew all about. I immediately felt relaxation creeping into my body.

Yes, I felt right at home and began to relax.

Relaxing and getting away from my daily routine, I would find, was a key to what came next—a key, in fact, to the portal of my soul.

Maria Renata, itself, was a larger building than I had imagined. Years ago it had been a home for those recovering from Tuberculosis and was owned by a doctor. More recently, it was owned by the Sisters of the Resurrection who loaned it out to our diocese a few weeks a year for retreats.

The dining room was large, as was the living room/lounge area, both being graced by a long row of windows which allowed the sun's rays to spill across its wooden floors. The rectangular building seemed to curve around the shore of Lake Placid where I could see a dock and boathouse.

I had arrived early, as I usually did for appointments and such, and no one seemed to be nearby. So, I moved out the front door and made my way down to the water. There I decided to sit on the soft green grass that edged the lake and closed my eyes. *Help me to remain open to Your will*, I thought. I knew I needed to somehow come away from this retreat feeling of more worth than I had the last thirty-eight years of my life.

Of what worth are you?
Of what worth am I?
How do we know?
I asked with a sigh.

What have I earned?
What do I deserve?
My mind answered softly,
Deny is the word.

This was odd. I'd come here feeling I needed time to relax and think about my life. But what was surfacing from somewhere deep inside my soul was a feeling that I was *not* worthy.

Why? I wondered. *Did I usually feel this way?* Thinking back, a recent incident leapt to mind.

A few months before, I'd found a skirt that I fell in love with at first glance. It was even my size which didn't happen very often. As usual, I had talked myself out of buying it. My mind was telling me that I didn't *need* it, that I didn't have the *extra money* to buy it.

But at the same time, I knew that *denying* myself the purchase went deeper than that—*a lot* deeper.

Centering on the feeling I had, holding the skirt in my hands, it was this: I didn't feel I *deserved* it. I felt I had to earn the right to make the purchase, as if it was a reward. I hadn't done enough—enough of what, I didn't know—in order to deserve it.

For the first time, sitting there at Maria Renata, I became aware that feelings I carried with me could have deep roots, much deeper than I was aware of.

Where did such feelings originate?

Keeping myself in the moment of reverie, I let my thoughts drift back . . . and back . . . and before long, an incident from long ago entered my mind and stirred my heart.

From the early days, my family struggled. There was never enough money, much less any extra. We all knew that. It seemed that my parents argued over money all the time.

When the money ran out, which came from dad's savings and the cashing in of insurance policies, he joined a carpenters' union and began to work. My early memory of him is his working away from home most weeks, traveling home on weekends. Every year, he was only able to get enough work to qualify for unemployment. So, things were tight money-wise. Every penny was counted. Nothing could be wasted, and no extras were allowed.

The house always carried a sense of tension. Or maybe the tension was in us.

During my early years, I, of course, grew into my sister's clothing. That is what I wore. With my oldest sister living and working back in the city, my next to the oldest sister, six years older than I, benefited from her purchase of pretty skirts which she would bring with her when she visited. I couldn't wait to grow into them, few as they were.

Now, there was a small independently owned dress shop in town on the main street. Mom would sometimes make a purchase there, saving her money from the grocery money given to her as rent by my brother who boarded at our house. He had a job working in a nearby town. Dad didn't give her any money for groceries. My brother's rent money purchased all of our food, outside of what Mom raised and canned from the garden. That money also paid for all the paper goods, personal care items and clothing.

Dad's money contributed to the fuel bills, telephone, electricity, car expenses and the mortgage. Any medical bills were an added burden. Fortunately, we were quite a healthy bunch.

One day, when I was in sixth grade, Mom and I found ourselves walking down the main street of our little town. We had been doing some grocery shopping and had placed the packages in our blue and white Hudson with the extra tire encased on the back. As we moved down the street, Mom guided me to the dress shop.

"Let's go in here," Mom said. "We have to get you a coat for winter this year."

"A coat? For me?" I found it hard to contain the excitement I felt.

This was a new experience for me. I couldn't believe it. *A new coat . . . all mine*! I felt a bubbling up inside of me and then a barrage of bursting like fireworks on the Fourth of July. Mom opened the door and we entered. *What would the coat be like*? I wondered. *Would I like it? Would I have a choice?*

I had been in the dress shop a few times before when Mom wanted to check on what they were carrying or needed to buy something minor like a slip or underwear. The owner was a tall woman with short black hair. She was always friendly and gave me special notice. I liked her eyes. They told me *"I like you."* before she even spoke a word.

"How are you today, Rose, and how are YOU Debby? Is school going well?" she inquired.

"Oh, yes," Mom replied. "We're very well, thank you. We're looking for a coat for Debby. Do you have any in her size?"

"Well, let's look over here and see," she said as she guided us to the left side of the long, narrow store.

There, all the coats were neatly arranged with the sizes boldly marked. The adult sizes hung on the rack up above with the children's coats hanging down below them.

"I'll be over by the blouses while you look," she said. "Try on any you wish to and let me know if you need any help. Our new shipment just came in so I'll be over there arranging blouses." She drifted away and left us to our own exploration.

I stood there, looking at the rack, my eyes traveling carefully down the row. My eyes passed by the black one, the brown one, the dark green one. Mom was moving through them, looking at the sizes and, of course, the prices. All of a sudden my eyes stopped, fixating on the coat I saw right in front of me.

"Oh, Mom, look at this one," I said, desire written all over my face. "It's beautiful and so soft . . . "

The coat was a light beige-colored heavy corduroy with a thick, off-white downy pile lining. Even the hood featured that soft fluffy layer of pile. It made me feel like I was stroking pure velvet. I loved it!

"Why don't we try it on?" she said. As I slipped my arm inside the sleeve, I could feel the pile lining secure itself around me as if it were a very part of me. It was a truly marvelous feeling of being snug, safe and secure, like I was wrapped up in a cocoon that was protecting me from all that was unhappy in my life. I stood there, looking in the mirror.

"It fits!" I exclaimed, not daring to hope too much. "It even has room for me to grow into," I added.

Mom didn't say anything in reply. I watched her as she walked over to the owner and began speaking with her. My breath caught in my throat. *Could she be making arrangements to buy the coat? Was it possible that this coat was going to be mine? All mine?* I realized that that was exactly what she was doing, making arrangements to pay off the cost of the coat, dollar by dollar, week by week. I knew Mom had done that before with things she needed to purchase, and the owner was so trusting of her. I was all jittery inside. I just couldn't believe it. I couldn't wait to wear that coat. *It was new! It was mine!*

Upon returning home, the tide began to turn. The atmosphere seemed to grow heated as we walked through the front door. I could sense the tension in Mom. What was it?

"What did you buy?" demanded Dad, a condemning sound in his voice.

"A coat for Debby," Mom quietly responded.

"How much did it cost?" he asked. His untrusting tone remained.

I turned away and quickly moved down the hall to the room I shared with my sister. The air was now boiling and ready to blow. The tension was mounting to full bore. I didn't hear Mom's quiet response. I held my breath as Dad erupted, fear shooting through me.

I threw myself on my bed, contracting within like a rubber band that had been stretched to the infinity of joy and pleasure and then released to snap back to a state of full constriction.

I buried my face in my pillow as I heard him yell, "What are you, crazy? It goes back!"

And back it went. I never got to wear it. It never came out of the box it had so delicately and neatly been placed in at the store. It just disappeared. No one even told me about it or explained why. And I knew not to ask what had happened to it.

I felt like I wasn't worthy of that coat—that coat with a price tag on it. *Yet*, I wondered, *how do I become worthy? How do I become valuable enough to deserve that coat? Is it even possible? Maybe I am really selfish,* as my sister had told me many times, *desiring something I didn't deserve just because I wanted it. Guess I'm not worth the money. Shame on me.*

The next weekend, Mom, Dad and I traveled to a discount store in a nearby town. There we found a brown coat that fit me, for a discounted price. I thought it was ugly but I knew not to speak a word. I felt guilty that I had been the cause of Mom getting yelled at again. *It was my desire for the coat that was to blame. I was responsible. Well, I'm not going to desire something warm and soft and beautiful for myself anymore.* And that was that.

After the purchase was made, Dad rushed us out of the store. We got in our blue and white Hudson and quickly drove away.

"That clerk misread the price," he said while he gloated. "She charged us even less."

I felt sick inside. I felt like we'd stolen that coat, that ugly coat. Why weren't we just returning to the store and offering to pay for the coat at the correct price? Isn't that what being honest is all about? *I will never do that myself. I will always try to be as honest as I can.* So, now, I was only worthy of an ugly, brown, *stolen* coat.

I would wear that coat, always remembering that soft, beige, pile-lined corduroy coat that had given me such a warm, safe feeling. I had lost a lot of respect for my dad that day. Would I ever get it back? And what about my own sense of worthiness? I felt that my soul had shrunk yet another degree in the arena which would become my life.

That had happened a long time ago and, yet, I could remember everything about that incident. Was I still carrying that feeling of not being worthy of the warm pile-lined corduroy coat? And was I transferring that feeling of unworthiness to other parts of my life? What about believing that I am *worthy* of true love? What about feeling that I *am* loveable? And then the final question—Am I *worthy* of being healed of Multiple Sclerosis?

There were a lot of questions I needed to find answers to during this, my first, retreat and maybe I wouldn't find many. *If I could just find one answer, that would be a good place to start.*

I had selected my spiritual director from a list of unknowns using my intuition. Father Fred was a Jesuit from New York City and very wise. He was in his late seventies, I believe, and had lots of experience in spiritual direction. His gentle, relaxed manner put me at ease immediately. He became my confidante in minutes and was responsible for much of my growth during that retreat.

Although the retreat was held in silence except for daily mass and a daily conference with my spiritual director, I learned so much about the other participants. Without conversation, it surprised me.

It didn't matter what their names were or where they were from. Their habits, the way they carried themselves, what they selected to eat and how they ate spoke volumes to me. Where they chose to meditate or to write explained a lot about the persons they were. Where they chose to sit or walk or what time of day they were out and about were also clues to their identities. I realized that I was *very* comfortable with the silence.

Father Fred and I spoke of my inferiority complex in high school, how I had felt insecure much of my life, afraid to step out on my own. Yet, I wanted to. I *needed* to.

I began to share with him about my upbringing and my pain. And so I began.

Over my growing years, I came to realize that I was, in essence, on my own. It had been a slow cumulative effort formed from situation after situation, experience after experience. Though I was housed and clothed, I didn't feel like I was understood or maybe even loved that much.

Over and over I learned the lesson: Don't bother asking. Why ask for something when the answer would probably be "No"? And the "no" always caused a deep hurtful feeling inside me, like a knife cutting all the way to my heart. So the message was clear: Do without. Sacrifice. That's where my natural sense of sacrifice came from.

When my husband told me, after the children were born, that I didn't have to go back to work *if* I could budget our expenses and pay for them on his income alone, that sealed it. It sealed me.

What had previously been my relaxing, fulfilling hobbies, things like crafting, cooking and baking from scratch, gardening and canning, then became a scorecard on which I could record pass or fail. It meant making all my own cards because I didn't want to ask my husband for money. It meant growing as many of my own foods as possible to control the chemical fertilizers and pesticides my family ingested and to save money. It meant taking time to wash, dry, and reuse plastic bags to aid the environment and also to, guess what?—save money. All of this I had done previously for enjoyment but now it had become a requirement to stay at home with my children.

Now I had an intense need to make EVERY card I wished to send, EVERY meal I needed to serve, EVERY item I wished to bake and wash EVERY bag I had used. At one point, I was making all of our breads—loaves of whole grain bread for sandwiches, bagels, English muffins, Italian bread, rolls for dinner and cinnamon raisin bread for toast. Yes, it was healthy for the family, but the energy I put into this was more than what one puts into a hobby.

I felt driven by a need so intense and deep that it nearly consumed me.

If I didn't get the bread made on a given day, I felt that I'd failed. If I didn't get every card made that I felt I needed to, again, I had failed. When I was deep into the project of sewing some clothes for the girls, I would set a due date for completion in my head. It became automatic to do so and to organize my time, to plan, to . . . there's that score card again . . . pass or fail.

What began as an interest, perhaps a hobby, and a joy, eventually became entwined with my identity. What I made was who I was. The fact that I saved money by not spending any to make my life easier said something about me. I was a good person because I didn't have needs that would cost anyone anything.

I had become a master budgeter in all respects, measuring not only money but the amount of time it *should* take me to do various tasks, the amount of time it *should* take me to get the errands done, the amount of time it *should* take me to clean the house, cook a meal, can the peaches, pears, tomatoes or applesauce. How had I figured the required amount of time? What standard had I used? It was all automatic.

I had set the standards for myself very high, I guess because I never felt that what I did was ever good enough. I could always do better. My dad had never accepted my performance. It never was worthy of any praise from him, or at least that's how I saw it. Now *I* couldn't accept my performance, either. The effects of that would take years to show themselves.

The time with my girls was never budgeted, though. I wanted them to feel loved, to know they were important and of value. My time with them directed my whole day and I lavished them with it. At times, we made cards together and at other times they became my assistants in the kitchen, pouring ingredients into the bowl, or kneading their very own lumps of dough. Those were fun activities for all of us and I didn't feel as driven at those times. Those times had no expectations. Even the clean-up was fun. I wanted to stay at home with them and experience it all.

Sadly, each day ended with a list of what I had not gotten done. Somehow I never caught up, never felt I *could* catch up. It was like I was always on an invisible treadmill and the hill just got steeper and steeper, while my image of myself and my sense of value declined. I didn't complain about the noose that I felt had encircled my soul. It grew tighter day by day, month by month and year by year. *Please help me to endure.* My mom had endured her life as it was. I could, too.

Sacrifice had become almost second nature to me. It didn't matter that I didn't see any of my friends doing the huge list of tasks I attempted each and every day. That was me, pure and simple. My example had been my mom. Her life had been one of total sacrifice and I hoped to one day become the humble person I saw her to be. It seemed to me that she put everyone else's needs before her own.

I wondered if that was what I needed to do to become humble, to discount my own needs. I just didn't know how to get there at the time. I was not aware that life had already begun building a mighty basis for that to occur.

Given the fact that I felt of less and less value, a façade grew up around me, attaching itself without my being aware of it. On the surface, with this outer shell that I had acquired, I exuded an aura of independence and very little personal need. Yet, inside, I felt very needy indeed.

My shy, quiet demeanor in high school had kept me in the background, while my smile welcomed everyone to me. I had not been popular in school but was a good student with capabilities that rarely showed themselves. I had lost student council elections but had been voted Honorary Head Cheerleader my senior year by the rest of the girls on the squad. I had also been voted Miss Congeniality by the rest of the contestants at the County Fair Queen Pageant. I was pleasant and friendly to all.

My heart did house jealousies in high school. I envied girls from financially sound homes as I listened to them speak of family trips and the latest styles of clothes purchased for them. I envied the freedoms girls my age had to date and have boyfriends.

I felt like I didn't have much to share with them that would be of any interest. I envied them their happy homes.

Jealousy and envy are not pleasant feelings. I would try to bury them as soon as their angry heads were aroused, but burying them does not rid one of them. Consequently, as the cliques formed, I was not included.

I acquired two dear friends who continued to remain my friends throughout high school. With them, I could share my meager news. I knew that I was different from the other girls and yet there was an intuitive knowing that I was somehow also special. Those words, however, never reached my ears during my formative years.

In my class right before lunch, my stomach would sound its loud gurgling moans. It was truly embarrassing. My face would sear with heat and my gaze would drop to my desk. I wondered who could hear, and felt mortified every time my stomach rumbled.

I found a solution to my problem by carrying a package of Pine Brothers' cough drops with me to class. As I felt the hunger pains awaken, I would ease a cough drop into my mouth. It was soft and would adhere to the roof of my mouth. There it would stay, ever so slowly dissolving, giving my stomach just enough to suppress its embarrassing noises.

In that class, there was a boy I had a crush on who was quite popular. He sat near me and would motion to me to share my cough drops with him. I was thrilled to do so! But sharing cough drops would never win me his affection, much to my disappointment. He ended up dating one of the popular girls. My heart, once again, plummeted. These experiences of high school helped to solidify my low self-image.

It's no surprise then, given the façade I had built, that at twenty years of age I had attracted someone who was happy to have a woman in his life that didn't seem to need anything. He had responded to the unspoken message that I was unconsciously presenting to the world.

Soon after we were married, I had been able to share my deep needs with my husband, but he wouldn't even listen, much less *hear* what I was desperately trying to communicate to him. I had tried to become more physically attractive, even changing the style of clothes I wore, my behaviors and my reactions in whatever way I thought he wanted. But I couldn't change my needs.

Understandably, oil and water don't mix. There are times when they travel side by side, but they never blend, never join, never truly become one.

My husband was not an inherently bad person, though he was an angry one who had demons he didn't wish to talk about. He didn't seem to be capable of giving me what I needed, or understanding what that was, even after being told.

There were fun times as a family, enjoying our daughters, but we would never really be married to each other in the true sense. How could we be?

My husband didn't seem to even want to recognize the presence of *his* demons and I'd learned to bury all my *true* feelings so deeply in my soul that I lost sight of them. Yet, those suppressed energies of my buried feelings and needs would gradually make their presence known to me and to my world.

Much was shared with Father Fred over the eight days of retreat. I grew in my state of awareness, melting the tip of the iceberg, so to speak. He was my channel for forgiveness, helping me to see the stresses I was putting myself through and the exorbitant expectations I placed on myself.

A day before the end of retreat, as I lay face down on the dock, my eyes wandered to the sight below. Looking between the wooden boards, I caught a reflection of light. As I focused more closely, I could see moss growing there, lush and green, obviously thriving. Yet, no one would notice it, no one *could* notice it, unless she was looking for it. But there it was, doing quite fine, serving its purpose in the scheme of things. Inconspicuous though it was, it was *not* insignificant.

That was the culmination, *my* culmination of this retreat. I was like that moss, growing lush and green in an obscure place. I was serving *my* purpose, though I wasn't sure I knew, yet, what that was. Now I just had to *believe* it. Could I?

Father Fred had asked us each to find a stone and bring it to our final gathering at the retreat. The stone I found was small yet its sparkle caught my eye. The sparkle of the stone made me think of a smile, *my* smile, and how it could cheer people.

"Debby, you are a light in the darkness," a near stranger told me.

When my smile cheered others, I felt great joy inside. My stone itself was small and inconspicuous but *not* insignificant, like the moss under the dock that no one sees but is as purposeful as any because it *lives*. It's *alive*. I began to see others in a different light. As far as those people I had difficulty dealing with, I knew I might need to focus, at the very least, on the fact that they were living breathing human beings. No matter what we disagreed about, that belief would help me to be able to respect them still.

I didn't think that I would view myself as insignificant any longer. I *was* comfortable with being inconspicuous, at least for now.

I noticed many rough edges on my stone. It made me think of the many scars in me that needed healing, both physically and emotionally.

Though I didn't know it at the time, much more lay ahead in terms of my need for an inward journey—a journey that would become more unsettling and harrowing.

6

ONCE UPON A ROCK

I t was the following summer. The year was 1989. I had taken a break and left Maria Renata where I was on my second eight-day silent retreat. Since last summer's retreat, I had noticed in myself a calmer outlook on life.

My relationship with my husband had not changed much. I kept trying to be the person he seemed to want me to be, which I could never quite live up to, but I had begun to look at myself in a more positive light. My quiet way and manner were characteristics of who I was and that was okay. I was beginning to accept that. I was beginning to accept *myself.*

I was drawn to climb a mountain on this retreat. The pull was strong. I attached my belt and connected my water bottle to it. I was off. My water, a packed lunch and my guide book accompanied me.

I took the ascent step by step around coarse granite boulders, over knobby roots worn smooth by erosion. Higher and higher, I progressed. I had never before climbed Porter Mountain, one of the 46 High Peaks of the Adirondack Mountains of New York State. Yet, here I was and loving it.

Climbing, to me, was a journey every time. I likened it to living my life. Climbing each mountain was a struggle, tiring and challenging. But if tackled step by step, with perseverance and determination, the reward was reaching the top and whatever surprises that held when I got there. It was like taking my life one day at a time.

Even if there wasn't a gorgeous view, the journey was worth it. I had accomplished my goal. Somehow, I knew the journey I was on in my life would be worth it, too, even if the finale wasn't gorgeous and fulfilling. It was worth it because I would have grown through the experience I'd had.

That was what I was all about—growing and learning more about myself and my world.

Even if I found myself in a cloud when I reached the summit, as I had on Tabletop Mountain, nature's brilliance, beauty and variety surrounded me. I was totally engulfed, becoming one with the cloud. I felt no division of any kind. It was a special moment that I had been blessed with and one I would never forget. I had felt complete—not alone, not disregarded. I had felt one with the universe . . . totally balanced . . . almost floating in the cloud I had become one with.

Here, as I struggled to reach the summit of Porter Mountain, I knew I was also struggling to find my purpose, to fulfill my life. What was it that I hoped to accomplish *this* time? What answers would I find?

As I neared the top, a huge boulder appeared on my left, coarse, grainy and crusted with gray-green lichen. The trail continued onward to my right, but I veered left, moving directly toward that boulder, drawn to it like a magnet to iron.

I carefully began circling the rock, looking for a foothold until a sufficient spot was found. Pushing with one foot, I pulled with my hands, first one and then the other, until I found myself atop the rock. Standing tall with only the air surrounding me, I slowly began to turn, my eyes wide with wonderment and surprise.

I'm above the tree line.

The view was breathtaking and I wasn't even at the top. This outcropping of rock placed me at the edge of a precipice so steep that I could not even view the bottom.

As I seated myself, my thoughts drifted again to my life and how I felt akin to this boulder. *Why is that? Why do I feel so connected here?*

I closed my eyes and let every muscle relax. It was a feeling of letting go. I likened it to a quiet opening up of the memory bank of the brain. All I could hear was the wind softly rustling the leaves on the bushes surrounding me. Then the scene was before me.

I saw myself as a child, moving through the forest behind the house where I grew up, to a place where I'd felt connected to all of Nature and to myself.

One spring day, I roamed the forest on one of my explorations. I must have been nine or ten years old. As I emerged from the deep woods and into a rolling field, I was drawn to a huge boulder at the top of a hill a little ways away, above a thick tangle of blackberry bushes. Hugging it was an ancient maple tree with branches extending outward and upward, stretching to the sky itself, as if it were hopeful in its quest for survival.

I needed to be on top of *that* hill, on top of *that* rock.

Charging up the hill, I reached the huge stone, and felt the coarse granular texture of it.

My fingers found indentations in its surface—places to grip with my hands and feet, so that I was able to climb to the top. In a moment I was standing on its domed crest, looking down the hill, over the blackberry bushes that abounded there, and surveying all of nature from my perch, right up to the forest edge.

This is my spot. Mine. And I'm queen of the world here.

That was when I noticed that the giant old maple had in its side a hollowed hole, where a limb had once been. Now it formed a secret place in the side of the tree—a *hiding* place.

I decided to keep a spiral notebook and pencil in it so that I could write my most private thoughts and record my creative urges.

Thereafter, every time I visited, I could reach inside my secret place from the top of my rock and pull out the treasures of my heart that I'd recorded and hidden there.

Since I had recently been exposed to poetry in school, I had become enamored with it. *Maybe I can create some poems,* I thought, *express my feelings that way.* I decided to call this my special place because I could go there to escape the arguments my parents had, escape the feelings of being different, and then there were also the feelings of being left out by my so-called friends. My emotions transformed themselves to written verse— the sadness, the fear, the hopelessness. I would always feel better afterward.

My rock supported me. It was solid. It was constant. It was always there. I could count on that. And the maple kept my secrets spilled out on paper. I thought, I felt, and I wrote. It was how I coped with my life back then—Nature and me, healing buddies.

Time, of course, moved on. I began to remember the day when I returned to that rock as an adult and how different everything was. The scene had changed dramatically.

Now my rock was *surrounded* by trees and they had grown taller than the rock itself. Some leaned over it, the lofty limbs of the white pine rested upon it.

I felt indignant at the view, realizing, right then, that I had expected it to remain the same, unchanged. And yet, I had changed, hadn't I? I was taller and had increased in weight so why hadn't I expected this scene to also respond to the passage of years?

The taller trees made my rock look different. It seemed much smaller. The scale for comparison had changed. That affected the atmosphere or the feel of my special place.

The openness that I had enjoyed as a child, sitting up there upon my rock, was now filled. The rock seemed as if it was being crowded out. As I adjusted to it all, I began to slowly approach my rock and circle it, finding the spaces and crevices to apply my hands and feet. Up I went, gripping and pulling. It didn't take long, now, before I was at the top.

As I sat down and looked around, I couldn't see down the hill to the forest anymore. It was as if the forest, in essence, had climbed the hill and was present all around me. The blackberry bushes that were so abundant years ago had died out. I felt crowded and enclosed. It wasn't comfortable at all.

As my disappointment took hold, I looked over at the ancient maple. It had become a hollowed out wormy, gray trunk, barren of any branches at all. It was totally dead. And I was witness to the beetle larvae having a hay day, reducing more and more of the wood to fine dust, Nature's life cycle in process.

Then I looked inside the trunk, I guess expecting to see my notebook there. Surprise! Had I *really* expected it to still be there? It had been fifteen years!

I had graduated high school, gone on to college and even earned my Master's Degree. Why had I expected Nature to remain the same? In a flash, I knew why; because Nature had always been a positive experience for me. I wanted to return to my rock *that* day and once again experience that grounded feeling, that support, that constancy I had once found there.

When writing my poetry upon that rock, I had felt free and renewed as I sat grounded and connected to Mother Earth. The words just seemed to flow out of me back then.

I *wanted* that feeling, again. I *needed* that feeling again, that feeling of freedom.

Realistically speaking, maybe the rain had softened the pages as the tree aged and they had disintegrated or animals had scavenged the paper. Birds may have used some remnants to line their nests. At this point, I could only surmise, but the notebook was part of the past, as were my childhood years.

The tree no longer showed the vibrant life it had when I first discovered it. The bark had become cracked and striated, broken, weary and lifeless in all dimensions, so different from my memory of it as a life-giving presence for my creative efforts.

The rock and the maple tree had become symbols of my renewal and refreshment at that young age and had continued well beyond those years to my present life. They would always be an inherent part of who I was, a being who needed to grow, yearning for security and searching for that experience of being grounded.

Sitting on this rock on the slope of Porter Mountain, I felt safe. I felt secure. Yet I knew that I would have to leave this rock and then the old feelings of being unsure of myself, who I was and what I was about would drop like a weight, pushing me down. Uncertainty occupied the inner chambers of my being. On the outside I seemed to have it all together, but inside was another story.

I began to creep cautiously to the edge of the rock, pushing my outer limits. It was a natural feeling for me to feel on the edge, like at any moment I might fall off. The question I'd ask myself was "and then what"? The great abyss yawned before me, risky and scary. The land around the rock was safe and secure as was the rock itself. Was I willing to take the risk? The risk of finding out *who* I really was?

I'd always thought of myself as someone uncomfortable with taking risks. If I were driving myself to an appointment in an unfamiliar place the following day, I would check it out a day ahead to be sure that I knew the way. In my teaching, I would rehearse the lesson plan over and over, well ahead of the time of delivery.

I thought back to my deteriorating marriage. I didn't feel I had a choice there. I had been taught that marriage was for life. The examples around me bore witness to that teaching. My mom and dad were a perfect example. Mom had endured it all, so I should be able to. *But should I? Could I? Why do I have such a difficult time with taking risks?*

As I sat there, feeling the breeze kiss my face and the warm sun cast its rays all about me, I began to relax and drift. My heart was no longer pounding inside me from the exertion of my climb. All was quiet except for the sound of the wind jostling some random leaves that dressed nearby bushes. My mind grew quiet and I saw myself as a little girl, playing beneath the white cedar tree.

The little girl was happy, playing with her dog, swinging on the board swing. Suddenly, she was crumpled up and sobbing her eyes out on the ground beneath the tree. What had happened in between? As I frantically searched my memory bank, nothing came to the fore. The heart-wrenching sobs continued and I began to cry, tears cascading down my face. I was one with the scene. I was feeling her pain. And then I realized . . . that little girl was *me*. My heart was pounding and I noticed I was sweating profusely. There was so much missing in the scene, so much I didn't remember, so much I didn't understand.

I knew this scene would play itself over and over in my mind until I made more sense of it, until the complete memory appeared. I hoped it would be soon. For now, I tried to let it go. Now was *not* the time to dwell there.

Unlike me, I wanted my girls to feel safe and secure in their home. There would be support, encouragement and lots of love. I never wanted them to doubt the love, at least from me. I had developed the belief that children who felt supported, encouraged and loved beyond a doubt by their parents, would have a strong base for becoming whoever and whatever they were to be.

I recalled that the Myers-Briggs Personality Inventory showed that someone with my personality characteristics ran a great risk of developing an almost co-dependent relationship with her offspring. That would not be healthy for either mother or child.

All of a sudden, I knew. I could see what was happening with me. I was beginning to depend on my girls to define my purpose. In so doing there was a definite possibility that I could make both of them become totally dependent on me for defining *their* own purposes. That would certainly not be healthy for any of us and could, in the long run, cause disappointment, hurt and pain for each of us.

I was the adult here and it was up to me to foresee that possibility and take the necessary steps to shift gears and get my needs met in other, healthier ways. I didn't know what those other ways were then, but I knew that my awareness would give me the motivation to find out.

The word "guide" flashed across my visual screen.

"Yes," I said with a sigh. "I am their *guide*."

With that, I dug out my pen and journal from my backpack. Opening to a new page, I let my heart speak to me . . .

Once upon a rock I sat
With trees surrounded there,
A quandary in my heart, I felt
Enveloped by the air.

My offspring had become my life
But naught was that to be,
For neither they nor I would gain,
Only withered be.

My role for them took clarity,
And then I felt at peace,
I was to be their guide I saw,
Not possessions would they be.

I could not cling to them for love
For that would harm us all.
Their spirits were not mine to own
For freedom was their call.

I was to guide that spirit growth,
Wherever that might lead,
Support, love, encourage them,
A true guide was I to be.

And so I left my rock on high,
Upon that mountain top,
And down I came renewed in love
And faith that could not stop.

It all became clear to me as I rested there upon the rock. I had been trying to be the perfect mom when the girls were young, overcompensating for what I had missed from *my* parents. As a result, I had gradually become driven in *all* aspects of my life. I was always striving to be the perfect mom, perfect wife, perfect friend and perfect teacher.

I recognized now what I was doing to myself. Since I could *see* the perfect way, I had been driving myself to perform at a very high level, in each role I filled.

To *see* perfection and not *pursue* perfection meant that I had failed. To *see* perfection and *not accomplish* perfection also meant that I had failed. With no one to support and encourage me in my adjustment to accepting a less than perfect standard, the voices in my head had a field day. *Who are you trying to kid? You'll never reach it. You'll never be. You are not worthy.*

My husband did not make a practice of expressing pride in me for anything I accomplished, so, as with my parents, that meant I had to try harder and harder. It was as if I was in a race and, yet, the finish line was impossible to reach. I was on a continual treadmill and the grade kept increasing. Increasing to where? Well, I guess I had found out. The race had stopped. The treadmill had come to a halt. I had developed a chronic illness.

I had been a needy Mom. All that was about to change. Now I could focus my attention on helping the girls experience some independence in their growing.

As they were beginning to babysit, I was going to encourage them to divide their pay, *saving* some each time and keeping the rest on hand to spend when they wished. The *saved* monies they could use toward clothes when we went school shopping, making some of their own selections. That would be the beginning. I would have to give the final approval as parent, but *they* could choose.

By the end of retreat, I felt that I was able to try again as far as my marriage was concerned. Maybe my husband had really missed me this time and would be more affectionate. That was my hope. Even if he wasn't, I felt I had grown stronger. I was evolving. I could feel it. But what would that mean?

7

A PLACE TO JUST BE

Fall arrived. One sunny day, I made my way to Bog River Falls which was located outside of Tupper Lake, in the center of the Adirondack Park, where I was living at the time.

The problem was, I didn't feel very sunny. I came here seeking peace . . . solace . . . answers. I was struggling once again. This was so old. Could I ever be free of these darker feelings that could drag me down, even on a bright, warm day surrounded by pristine mountains and lakes under a sky of brilliant blue?

I carefully parked my car in a forest pull-off. As I stepped out, the thunderous roar of the falls drowned out any other sounds.

Moving down the short path, I could feel a current of moving air caused by the rush of the water as it raced over the falls. The falls themselves were comprised of many interlocking pieces of granite—great slabs of rock that had been worn smooth by the force of river water moving over them season after season, year after year, and the rising and lowering of springtime water levels. Flooding had brought with it limbs and tree trunks that had either lodged against certain boulders or scraped over others, creating more drama as water coursed around and over them. The scene of the water, the trees, the rocks—everything was shining and shimmering in the sunlight that glinted everywhere. Silken waves of shallow water glided over the smoothed open bedrock closer to the bank, smothering what lay below it. What a contrast to the turbulent surging of the falls!

I hesitated there, feeling the strength, the force of the water that rushed along as if it knew its purpose, knew where it was going and where it was *supposed* to go.

What's my purpose? What good am I in this world? There I was again, surrounded by beauty and feeling pointless on the inside. Where did this feeling of being worthless come from? It seemed like it was always there, lurking in judgment in the back of my mind, waiting for an opportunity to once again whisper in my ear.

I could feel the circulating air that the rushing water produced, as it blew across my face, tossing my long brown hair about my shoulders. I closed my eyes and let myself become a part of it all. I inhaled the strength, the surety with which the water moved. I felt the peace and calm the breeze created, and for the moment I found that peace, too.

How I wished I could hold onto this sense for more than moments.

Picking my way carefully down the steep, stony bank, I approached an inlet of the river, a small feeder stream meandering through to its destination. I seated myself at its mossy edge.

I was in sight of the falls' beginnings, yet away from the most forceful part of the current. It evoked a scary sensation within me. I found myself acutely aware of both the life-*giving* quality of the water, which we need to survive, and the life-*taking* ability that it also had, as many unwary people had drowned in its swell.

I sensed there was a lesson here for me. As turbulent as it was at the surface of the falls itself, I saw nothing but smooth calm peaceful water far below this point, where it emptied out into the lake. It was also like that above the falls. And I thought about life—how I'd heard about people who go through rough waters in their lives, yet, in time, they navigate those difficult currents and peace becomes possible.

How do they find that kind of peace? I wondered. *How can I find it?*

A thought invaded my mind.

Stones, logs, and wind rile the water, but afterward, the water returns to the calm, placid state it always held. Like this water, some people are able to regain peace after turbulence, a peace that was there all along. Some people can just allow that to happen and it does. But some of us—like me—cling to old turbulences long past.

I had been through my own private storm, my own private tragedy years before. I had miscarried my third child. I came here seeking peace, solace, answers. *That's* why I was here. I began to see that I had found, in the turmoil of the falls and the quiet calm of the water at its base, a visual depiction of my tragedy and hope for the future.

As I sat at the mossy edge of the stream, I recalled another stream I had sought out when I was much younger, whenever I had questions. There I'd first found my solace—and sometimes my answers. How ironic that I had *again* been led to a stream in the forest in my quest.

I allowed my mind to drift back to another time, another place. The same question had plagued me then. *Why?*

In my adolescent years, I began to dread my return home from school each day. I still felt drawn to the forest. Nature remained my refuge from the darkness that I felt surrounding me. There, I didn't disappoint anyone and didn't have to keep pleasing anyone. I could just be.

And so, I was drawn to a new place for my solace, deep in the woods. A stream rushed through this arena of quiet and peace. The only sounds were those of rushing water, twittering chickadees and shouting blue jays with consoling air circulating through the immense white pine branches.

There, I sat, observing the water swirling over and around the rocks, gushing and rushing to who knew where. How appropriate, since I was in the stressful whirl of adolescence and craved the peace and quiet which this spot exuded.

The forest path to my special place was familiar to me, the big old pines hugging the path of pine needles, so soft and cushioning under foot. It gave me a feeling of warmth and comfort. Sometimes I felt like flying down that path with excitement and joy bursting inside me, though it seemed like years since I'd felt that way.

I had thoughts, many thoughts, as I sat upon the pine needle covered rock at the creek's mossy edge. I was like a sponge soaking up the green growth surrounding me, so vibrant, so simple and natural in its purpose, soft and secure. I gave this place a special name, 'A Place to Just Be', and I saw myself differently there. I felt calm and confident, as if I could face any problem and find a solution while I sat by the stream.

Why couldn't I carry the feeling this place gave me about myself *away* from this place? Why was it that the moment I was around other people, I felt like I was bumbling along? The good feelings would vanish.

Watching the water swirl around the rocks made me think of fingers, stroking and caressing each one before moving on to the stillness of the deeper bends in the stream. I yearned for that calm in my life. I felt left out so often and I was becoming more and more aware of being different from my classmates. I yearned to feel accepted, approved of and praised, and at the same time, I felt painfully guilty and ashamed that I had such a need.

I reached down and let my fingers linger in the cool flow of the stream, dipping them deeper and deeper. I felt the shame a lot, it seemed. Then there were my parents' arguments. I felt like I'd been dealing with this same issue all my life, but now it seemed to occur more often, much more often.

My parents' arguments were always about money—the lack of it, how it had been spent or how it should be used. I used to think, *Will the yelling ever end?*

I found myself staring at the saplings that stood so erect on the opposite bank of the stream. They were stretching and reaching toward the light. These saplings had their own challenges. The storms might wreak havoc with their leaves and branches. Droughts could drain their energies while rains could drown their roots. Diseases could attack them and threaten their very existence. I found my thoughts drifted to the old oak trees and the sturdy maples and how strong *they* became with time. As I sat there I knew that although I was as young as those saplings, I would someday be as strong as the old oaks and maples.

I would survive, too.

How? I wondered. *How am I going to get through life on my own, if no one likes or accepts me?*

In the silence, a thought appeared. *I have to take a first step. Well, maybe I have.* Suddenly I said out loud, "I've found a place where I can be myself."

My voice sounded strange to me—confident and strong. Those were qualities I had never thought I possessed but *always* admired in others. Yet, *here* I had found my voice.

As I looked up, I saw my collie dog, Lady, coming toward me, tired and panting. She walked into the stream, lapping up the water and sloshing around. Stepping out of the current just downstream from me, she shook herself then came closer and lay down, looking at me with her soulful eyes.

I ran my fingers through her wet sable-colored fur on the top of her head. She blinked, holding my gaze. How interesting that she should show up right at this moment, when I was struggling inwardly between feeling like I belonged and feeling like I belonged nowhere. Or at least nowhere but here, alone, by a quiet stream.

I felt she understood me better than anyone, maybe even better than I understood myself. Somehow she always managed to show up when I needed someone to be with me. Her constant presence and consistent support were like pillars that buoyed me up to face the world . . . *my* world, again.

I would never forget my place by the stream, the seat of pine needle covered rocks at the mossy edge of the creek.

Now, sitting by *this* stream, the dark voices that always returned were rising within me again. As if grief was not bad enough, there was an edge of accusation. *Why* did the miscarriage happen? Was I being punished?

Maybe I did something wrong and didn't deserve to have another child.

Suddenly I felt a sense of weakness coming over me. My bones and even my spirit felt weak.

With that feeling—not a new one, but a very old one—I remembered . . .

I had taken a bike ride a few days after discovering that I was going to have another baby. Bicycling down that country road, I was overcome with emotion. Pregnancy was supposed to be a blessing. At least that's how I had viewed my previous two pregnancies. But I didn't see, perhaps *couldn't* see how *this* pregnancy could be a blessing. *Where would the energy come from to give this child the love and security it deserved?*

I felt like the well of my soul was drying up. I was doling out love but I didn't feel the return, except from my girls. More was going out than was coming in and that had been the case for many years. This time, my pregnancy had elicited feelings of being trapped, trapped for another eighteen years before this child would graduate.

Maybe then I can rid myself of this loneliness I exist in almost every day, I'd thought. I had reached the end of it all and couldn't take it anymore.

Was that the way my mom had felt when she discovered that she was pregnant with me, this same vacant, desperately trapped feeling? Would God ever forgive her? Would He ever forgive me for not welcoming this new creation?

She had also been in a relationship that lacked the loving affection and care she so desired. Plus, she was living in a tiny space with no running water or reliable source of heat. She did have the love of her children. That helped her to survive until the time came to let go of them as they each left home to begin their own lives.

I found myself in a similar situation with this pregnancy. Sure, I had the convenience of indoor plumbing and heating, and my girls *could* supply a lot of love. But could I endure whatever lay ahead in what seemed to me a marriage without love? I wasn't sure.

One day not long after the bike ride, I felt slippery tissue passing out of me. At first, I didn't understand what was happening. I called the hospital and spoke with an obstetrician I had never before met, though a future appointment had been scheduled. He wanted to see me right away and a request was made to bring any passed tissue with me. My breathing became very shallow. I felt in a daze.

I needed my husband to offer words of comfort. I needed him to care for me and for our child.

I lay there in the examination room while the sonogram was performed. The obstetrician gripped my hand as he watched the screen with the technician. The sonogram showed a vacancy.

"There's nothing there," said the technician.

A deep sadness enveloped me. Tears streamed from my eyes. *My baby—was there nothing left?*

I was scheduled for a D & C the next morning. I sent my husband away to sleep elsewhere that night. I couldn't take his silence anymore. There was no comforting nor holding offered me. Why was he there at all? Was it because he *should* be? Awake in my room, in the quiet darkness, I sobbed.

As I lay in the hospital bed afterward, I asked my husband to cry with me at the death of our child. He wouldn't, or maybe he *couldn't*. Again, the loneliness was paramount for me. The more I counted on him for support and love, the expression of love that I so desired and needed, the further away I felt him drift.

As I sat by the stream at Bog River Falls, with life surrounding me and water flowing by, I realized what I was here to seek relief from—guilt. Had I somehow *caused* the miscarriage? At the end of the spectrum of possibilities, had my body ended the life of my own baby to keep me from being trapped?

I took a deep breath and recalled the words of my obstetrician. "You did not cause this miscarriage. A miscarriage is the body's way of ridding itself of an unhealthy fetus."

Why could I not allow myself to believe that? *Because part of me did not want to be pregnant again.* The dark voices inside raged against me with blame.

By now I had awakened enough in my personal journey to ask: *Where are these intense emotions coming from? Why am I always so quick to think that I must have done something wrong?*

Not only was I the one to blame for the miscarriage, I wasn't worthy to be the mother of the now-lost child, either.

But I had taken an important first step to finding peace again. I had come here to think, to listen, *to just be*, to let all unhealthy thoughts and feelings come, and then just go . . . sliding away, like the water over the falls.

I let them go now—the tangle of memories that included the miscarriage, the loveless marriage and my sense of being bad and unworthy.

In that moment, a thought came. My spiritual director had recommended I give my baby a name. Intuitively, I knew it had been a girl. Without hesitation, I knew her name.

"Your name is Kari Rose," I said. "And I love you."

Giving my baby a name gave her validity and value. She became my child, though I had neither any memory of her, nor had I shared any experiences with her. I had no pictures of her on photograph paper and none lived on in my mind. Yet, she was my child all the same.

That day, something deep and powerful happened. I had claimed a piece of myself by naming the daughter who'd been lost. It was as if I'd claimed an important piece of my *self*, as well.

Something in me shifted. I can't put into words how I knew, but I did. The healing of my body and soul had begun.

Finally, after decades, I was finally starting to move beyond the self-blame.

I was starting to become whole again.

8

BENEATH THE CEDAR TREE

Many months had passed since I completed my second retreat at Maria Renata. I had gotten through the first several weeks after the retreat, retaining a peaceful, patient demeanor but only *I* had grown. Bit by bit, the old stresses of our marriage claimed residence once again and I was unable to deter them. It seemed that the more I grew, the worse our relationship became. My husband had a great deal of pent up anger which he directed at me and I didn't appreciate it. I was beginning to feel as if I were a scapegoat for his frustration.

I became aware of a woman who was adept at assisting people with their childhood traumas. I knew there was a lot in my childhood that needed to be healed, so I made an appointment to meet her at her home.

I had arrived at this appointment with much trepidation. All I knew was that I needed to be there.

I felt as though I'd been led to this opportunity for healing, with someone who could help me seek and face buried memories, to encounter certain issues from my childhood that seemed to be pressing their way into the present, dragging me down emotionally and physically.

But did I really want *to remember? Did I really* want *to revisit difficult feelings from the past?* Doubt skittered through my mind. *Was it possible that something which happened to me so long ago could still be having an effect on me now, so many years later?*

I took a deep breath. *It was time to find out* because, in fact, I could sense that emotional scars laid down over the years, like soul sediment, had caused me to work harder and harder to prove . . . what? . . . to escape from a deep feeling of . . . again, what?

What was this nagging sense that lay so deep inside me? Somehow that feeling drove me to work extremely hard to show everyone that I was capable, competent, and self-sufficient; that I had no important needs. I had worked myself to exhaustion year after year until I'd run myself down and opened the door to disease.

What a perfect word for it: dis-ease, I thought, as in, the nagging sense *of never being at ease with my* self. But where had this feeling come from?

Again the thought came. *Do you really* want *to go back there? What about just letting it all go, and* moving on *from the past?* Another voice answered. *But what if the past won't let go of* you? Fortunately a third voice came to mediate. *You're an explorer and a seeker, a nomad of sorts. Give yourself the chance to explore your life and see if there are, in fact, doorways inside you that can set you free from the past.*

With that came resolve. I had long believed that if we allow ourselves to stay open, opportunities will always present themselves, through which we can learn and grow. If you are a seeker and a learner, new doors will always be there.

The question is—Do we *choose* to step into the new space that opens before us, mentally, spiritually, even physically? Or do we stay stuck, wringing our hands, not moving forward?

The choice is always ours. We can grow and change . . . or not change at all.

One of those doors faced me now. Was I willing to relive past pain? Was I willing to open up and look inside, sift through the layers of emotional sediment and gain insight into *why* I was the way I was—so sure I was without worth and so driven to work hard and, in that way, avoid the feeling of being worthless? Was I willing to look at who I was and what happened to me at the time certain traumatic events scribed on my soul the word 'unlovable'? Did I want to relive all that pain again in the hopes of finding a different way to see it, reinterpret it, and learn how to find now, in my adult life, what had never been given to me then?

I knew for sure that ignoring the pain did not make it disappear. It just redirected it into the cells and muscle tissue of my body. It continued to whisper there and sometimes shout. If I'd learned anything it was this: The body has a very long memory and years later it vividly let me know there existed in me very potent dis-ease.

Which memory would I be called upon to heal? Was it sane to knowingly cause myself pain or place myself in a painful situation on purpose, even if only in memory? I guess it all depended on the outcome.

It required trust, trust in the person who was there to lead me, and faith, faith that I would learn something from this experience. It was time to embark on the journey—*my* journey—through the layers of my life. If there was any chance that this would help me, I'd take it. So, I decided to give it a try.

I had met Kelly only once before, when out of curiosity and intrigue, I had scheduled a tarot card reading that she was doing at the home of a friend. I was met by a woman with rather long, straight brown hair which was pulled back and anchored behind her ears. She had the most insightful blue-green eyes I had ever seen. I was captivated and immediately calmed by her non-threatening, accepting manner. I was impressed by her *gift* and the way she spoke to me, throughout the reading, with clarity and compassion.

Afterward, I found myself scheduling another appointment, this time at her own home, as she was also said to be gifted in helping others in healing their childhood traumas. Again, I was curious and intrigued, wondering if that was the basis for *most* of my problems, particularly my disease. *How could that be?* I wondered. Yet, something was nudging me onward. Certainly, there was a lot of trauma within me in need of healing. However, I had always been a person who is more comfortable with some foreknowledge of what I was getting myself into. But, with that all said, I took on the challenge.

As I arrived at her compact cabin in the woods, I was immediately drawn by the welcoming setting. The surrounding trees and wildflowers spoke to me of peace and kindness. I later found out that she had designed and built the cabin herself. It was placed among the trees as if it was an essential part of the existing landscape. It was perfect.

As I got out of my car, she greeted me and led me into a very bright, yet quiet room, with light-filled windows facing me. We then climbed a wooden ladder to a loft area with large soft pillows decorating the floor. Calm and peace defined the space.

In a room dimmed of light, in a sanctuary of quiet, we sat on pillows, cross-legged and comfortable.

Kelly began by explaining Soul Loss, a Shamanic belief that when we experience a trauma, a fragment of our soul slips away in order to preserve itself.

One of the two places the missing fragment can be found is in an environment where the child feels fully supported as the creative being she is. There she feels safe to freely express herself.

The other place is where the trauma *occurred*, but here she is *ignoring* the trauma and occupying the time through a more enjoyable activity.

When a painful experience occurs, instead of trying to bury it or pretend it didn't occur, what we need to do is acknowledge it and cry it out. Otherwise, we grow into adulthood and our souls are not whole.

As the soul heals, the fragments return (Soul Retrieval) and the soul can eventually regain its wholeness. The Shaman's role is to "see" the trauma, find the missing soul part and convince it to return to the now-grown body, the original situation having changed. Upon its return, it can once again happily and safely express itself.

Between about five months before birth until eight years of age, a child believes that everything she sees, hears and feels is the real world. We carry these beliefs, behaviors and perceptions into our adult world. These form the basis of our adult pain and suffering until we realize that we only inherited them through our family and that we now have alternatives. We can choose to believe *something else* about ourselves.

Shamans understand Soul Loss as misplaced energy, likened to a groove in the neural pathways. The groove can be either created or sealed over by our adopted belief systems and behaviors. This action was determined by our awareness. It has been observed that some grooves close and new ones open when a belief is healed, resulting in a change in behavior.

Soul Loss feels like something is missing. We feel empty within, like a hole that can't be filled. Some try to fill the hole through eating, others through shopping. Some counter the emptiness with restless activities that fill each moment of their days. Still others escape through use of drugs and alcohol.

Modern-day physics explains this through the field of Epigenetics.

To say the least, I was awed by her words. *I can relate to this*, I thought. It made so much sense. Being a scientist at heart, I knew I was onto something. This was for real. There were answers ahead for me. I knew it.

"What is your intention for this session?" inquired Kelly.

Without any forethought, I answered her. "I want to feel of value, not worthless anymore." With that said, the intention was set.

Kelly guided me back to my *feelings* of worthlessness, lying way beneath the surface of my earliest memories . . . back . . . back . . . deeper . . . deeper. As I began to picture myself then, memories clustered around me like a warm fuzzy coat, lending me a comfort I rarely felt. As I allowed myself that feeling of comfort, one memory began to envelope me totally.

Suddenly I was *there*, at age seven, playing beneath the white cedar tree near the white wooden house where I grew up in the rural outskirts of Lowville, New York in the township of Watson. I allowed the scene to develop like I was watching a movie of my life. The scene became quite vivid—with the buzz of the cicada and even the pine scent of the forest surrounding our house.

A little girl with dirty blond hair and a smile written across her face was laughing and playing with her dog under the white cedar tree.

Keeping the visualization fresh in my mind, I began to speak, describing the setting, the feelings, the sensations, clinging to the description as if to life itself. The words just flowed out of my mouth like a script to a waiting audience.

"When I was a little girl, I loved playing outside under the white cedar tree that stood forty feet tall in front of our house, its lofty branches stretching outward. One of the lower branches supported a board swing which hung from it with thick twisted ropes. Slivers from that rough rope often housed themselves in my hands. Then it was time for Mom and her tweezers. Once they were removed, I was back at it again."

I felt calmness surrounding me as I continued. "Nothing could compare to the feeling I would get from swinging back and forth . . . back and forth, higher . . . and higher . . . until with one particularly forceful stretch, my toes just brushed some of the foliage of that tree which extended out from another limb higher up. *"Yes! I did it!"* I'd shout. A delighted feeling of accomplishment would rush through me, laughter spreading throughout my entire being. That was how I felt each time I was swinging, reaching the apex of my flight. Pleasure and pushing to the extreme coincided, side by side."

I paused, reveling in the positive feelings which that memory brought me. "Ah, yes. The breeze I would create with the force of my swing thrilled me, my hair flying out behind me. Then, just as forcefully, I would retreat backward as I descended on my return flight. My hair would reverse its position, zipping forward by my ears, momentarily obscuring my vision only to resettle again for my next forward swing.

The thrilling minutes flew by, as with a loud voice, I sang any song that entered my mind. The excitement and pure joy I experienced swinging on that swing . . . " My mind drifted. I was *feeling* each swing, back and forth. It was wonderful.

After a few moments, I went on. "Many times I would jump off that board swing and land in a pile of maple leaves that I had raked with this daredevil activity in mind. The pile would lie there, dry, crisp and inviting.

I loved to lie down in those leaves, smelling the fragrance of fall, those scents that say "Winter's approach is just around the corner." Scratchy though this felt on my skin, I would lie there as time passed, catching my breath after all my vigorous swinging.

Someone else enjoyed this pastime, too. My dog, Lady, would come romping up from somewhere, probably a nice cool shady spot down by the creek. She was a long-nosed, long-haired Scotch Collie with a gentle disposition. My brother had purchased her as a puppy for our family. Mostly, she was his and mine. She loved to tunnel through the leaves and would even let me bury her in them. Then she would erupt out of the pile with the leaves flying everywhere and pounce on me, licking my face.

She was happy. I was happy. Those were great days! And then it began to change."

I paused here, not wanting to leave behind the wonderful feelings I was having. I took a deep breath as I sensed a change in the atmosphere of my life back then.

"One fall afternoon, after my swinging, jumping and playing in the leaves with Lady, I realized how thirsty I was. I picked myself up out of the leaf pile and headed off to the house to get a drink of water, carefully brushing each fragment of leaf from my pink shorts and matching shirt. Pink really was my favorite color. I felt like a flower blossom when I wore it—pink and pretty, light and free. I stopped and bent over, giving my head some vigorous shakes. *There have to be leaves in there, too,* I thought. With that task accomplished, I entered the house, the screen door swinging shut behind me.

I was heading straight to the bathroom to get my drink, since that was the easiest faucet to use, when I heard my sister's voice. I turned toward the direction of her shout.

She was charging down the hall toward me from my parents' bedroom, their door ajar. She stopped abruptly as she drew near with a look of terror on her face. The eyes that focused on me were wide and glistening. The whites were vivid, surrounding the sky blue coloring of her eyes.

She assumed a posture that was straight as a board. Her arms hung stiff and long at her sides with fists balled up tightly, held close to her body. Her cheeks were red and shiny like she had been crying. Loud, choppy gulps of air that exuded fear escaped from her lips.

"Debby, what are you doing?" her tone frantic.

"I want a drink of water," I replied.

"Get it and go back outside," she directed as she tried to catch her breath. "And leave another cup of water here, at the end of the hall."

"What's going on?" I insisted, anxiety creeping into my stomach. Something was strange here, and scary.

"Just get it and go back outside!" she shouted as she turned around and began running back down the hall, back to my parents' bedroom.

I gulped a cup of water, left the other cup of water as she had requested and hurried back out the front door. But now, my curiosity spiked.

Quietly, I moved around the perimeter of the house until I found the windows of my parents' bedroom. I drew closer to a side window which looked open. I could hear Dad yelling. That wasn't a surprise to me. He seemed to yell a lot, mostly at Mom. But . . . *is that Mom lying on the bed?* I thought as I drew even closer. *Why is she so still?*

My sister had reentered the bedroom and Dad was yelling at her. "Whose tire tracks are in the driveway? Who was here?"

No word from Mom. She was just a still body, frozen on the bed. *Why isn't Mom speaking up, defending her daughter? Had he hit her? Had she fainted?*

"Mr. Muncey just gave us a ride home," my sister tearfully responded.

That's all I heard. The raging, accusatory tone in my dad's voice sent chills through me. The adrenaline rush of panic was unleashed. Something was wrong—worse than wrong—and fear took hold of me.

Jumping up, I ran back around the house, taking refuge beneath the cedar tree. Burrowing myself behind the tree trunk, I hid there and made myself as tiny as possible.

Tucked in a ball, I wanted to disappear forever, releasing sob after sob. The panic had given way to a sickened feeling in the pit of my being. *Did Dad think that someone else had visited? Did he think that Mom had done something wrong?* The truth of his thoughts and feelings was just out of reach for me at my age. But the rage in him and my mother's frozen being told me something horrible had happened . . . or didn't happen and my father thought it had . . . or *something*.

"I don't understand. I don't understand," I kept repeating out loud as the fearfully sickened, sad feelings wrenched through me. My body went into an even tighter frozen curl. A tremor shook my whole being. Everything was constricting, compressing inward. I felt all alone and totally vulnerable. I wanted to be anywhere but here. The tears streamed down my face as I sat there.

In another moment, if I didn't protect the center of myself, I felt I would be annihilated.

I felt so small . . . so unimportant . . . so desperately helpless. Hearing his words in that tone of voice, trying to get as far away from it as I could, escaping it, hiding from it, and not understanding what was going on brought on the monumental feeling of being totally overwhelmed by it all. *What was happening?* I could feel my heart constricting as I relived this part of the memory.

"The big deal Havases . . . big deal Havases," I repeated over and over. It came out of nowhere, but seemed to make sense right now as a sort of chant. I'd heard my mother frequently make that remark, disgustedly, Havas being our last name. She was referring to my father's attitude of being more important than he actually was—a 'big deal'.

It seemed that so much of what my father did and said, at this point in his life, was all bluff and bluster and show. He acted as though he was on top of everything, yet, we were really quite needy.

Every day my father went out into the world with a well-formed mask to hide the threatened, insecure man that he had become. As a young adult, he had been a rather skilled and secure person with aspirations and dreams. Maybe he was hoping that by playing the "big man" role now, he might recapture some of his positive beliefs for the future, or at least cover his failure.

Somehow, even at my young age, I knew the truth.

Tears coursed from my eyes. *What's happening to us? What will happen to* me?

Lady pranced over and began licking my face, her concern over my wretched state showing. I buried my face in her soft sable-colored fur, trying to make it all go away. I felt so overwhelmed."

Later, I would realize something was taken away from me that day, something very deep. The house of my childhood had been broken apart. The home of my soul had been threatened. It was a feeling of annihilation—a feeling that any deep sense of security I'd had was utterly destroyed in my home, my family and—*me*. I wasn't safe anymore. That safe place which I called "home" that I trusted to keep me safe and secure had collapsed. The carefree child I'd been vanished.

Now, in our room dimmed of light, in our sanctuary of quiet, we sat on pillows, cross-legged and comfortable. We listened to the stillness, with eyes closed, allowing the memory of that day and all of the events to emerge within me.

Reliving the fear and the deep pain of loss, I see my child-self beneath the white cedar tree near the white wooden house where I grew up. There, huddled against its rough-barked trunk, was little Debby, terrorized by what she had just experienced—her mother lying so still on the bed, her dad yelling, her sister in a frenzy, crying loudly. She didn't have anywhere else to go. She didn't understand what was happening. She felt helpless, responsible, and overwhelmed by it all.

I began to cry as I absorbed her feelings. I knew that this memory needed to be healed, the pain relived, the loss regained.

"I am here 100 percent with you . . . I am here 100 percent with you," Kelly said softly, over and over.

She instructed me to go over to the child, gather her up and give her a hug. I quietly enfolded the sobbing child in my arms, lovingly holding her, comforting her, supporting her. I felt myself absorbing her. Her tears were now my tears and they flowed together. I allowed myself to again experience that deep cavernous pain of loss. The minutes passed and as we cried together, Kelly directed me to speak to the child from my heart.

I began to speak to my much younger self. "You aren't helpless. You will grow and accomplish things. There will be a tomorrow."

I continued to hold the child close to me. I focused, transmitting all the love I felt into her, filling her emptiness with it, filling her hollow heart.

"I forgive you, Debby, for the pain I have carried throughout my lifetime," I told her. "I love you *so* much. *You* are beautiful."

I began to rock with her in my arms. "I am not helpless, I am not helpless, I am not helpless," I repeated over and over again, the words becoming my mantra.

Time passed. The sadness began to drift away. As I began to feel a lightness, it was quickly replaced with a heaviness on the right side of my heart. I again dropped down into my pain, as the tearing away of the painful shards of self-hatred fought to remain in residence there. Tears gushed from my eyes. And then . . . it was gone! The enemy had invaded but had not won. *I am not helpless. I am not worthless. I am of value. This I believe. And this I f-e-e-e-l!*

For long minutes, I felt the lightness returning. I opened my eyes, raising them up to the light streaming in delicate rays through the high, narrow window near me.

A smile crept across my face.

We sat quietly in the dim light. I felt the pain that I had carried my entire life melt away as a new current of tears slowly inched its way down my cheeks. The pain of the past carried within was no longer the source. It was the happiness of the present that refilled the empty place within my soul and rejuvenated my heart.

Something of vast importance had just happened. A love for my *self* had been restored within the depths of my soul. I felt resolution . . . and peace.

Over the next several months, I realized that the feeling of being overwhelmed when many things are presenting themselves at the same time in my life was no more. All those feelings of being helpless were replaced by feelings of comfort and sustainability. As far as understanding it all, can we ever understand it *all*?

The inner journey had begun. I knew that the intense agonizing desire to *have* to understand had been modified to a desirable curiosity. So, now I *wanted* to understand how and why it had all come about. Were there other events, concealed in layers of memory within me that shaped my beliefs about myself? If so, what effects were they having on me?

I no longer felt as driven in that arena of my life. The impulse to prove I wasn't worthless had been dealt a severe blow. It was like some neural grooves *had* closed and new ones *had* opened to allow for the changes I was experiencing. Healing had certainly taken place. But was there more? Could I experience more healing and more freedom from the past?

How comforting to realize that the white cedar tree that had brought me hours of joy and delight had also been witness to the feelings of annihilation and finally, my return to completeness.

For it was in visualizing myself beneath its branches, where at first I experienced my free spirit, and next sought refuge, that years later, I would find my respite there as well.

9

SHAME ON ME

The following summer I was again at Maria Renata in Lake Placid. It was my third eight-day silent retreat. I knew the area of my life that I was ready to deal with on *this* retreat—that of forgiving my father. I was finally ready to relive it all, though I knew it might be a journey filled with unpleasant memories. That was, unless there was something *else* for me to deal with instead.

I must try to stay open, I thought as I opened my car door and removed my pack. *My journey once again begins.*

Forgiving my parents was an awesome but necessary prospect. I had realized of late how confined I felt as I held onto regrets, hurts and the feelings of anger. There were so many inconsistencies and favoritisms doled out to my siblings while I was growing up and, of course, *injustices* as I saw them.

My parents seemed to have different values and philosophies of child rearing. Mom was patient and soft-spoken while Dad was strict and always yelling. Then there were the different discipline techniques. Dad was all physical, giving "lickings" with his leather belt or slipper, and Mom did her best to make me ashamed of myself for whatever I did do or didn't do that she felt inappropriate. There was also shame for what I said or didn't say, that she thought I should.

They did their best to stop the development in their children of that evil presence of pride. *That,* they agreed upon. No praise was given us, and little affirmation and support came our way except for my one sister who had been born premature. They both were very proud of her and, being younger, I heard it much of the time. When they spoke of her and her accomplishments their faces beamed, though I don't think even *she* heard it directly very often. When someone inquired after her, my parents informed them that she was studying to be a school teacher, pride bursting on their grinning faces.

Here I am, thinking about parents when I thought I was going to concentrate on my dad, I said to myself. But somehow my mind kept reverting back to Mom. *We'll just have to see,* I thought as I closed my car door and made my way down the walk I had come to know so well.

After settling in, I made my way down the trail to my favorite place. It seemed so familiar now. The bushes had grown a little taller, new grasses had sprung up along the way. There were more daisies blooming than there were at this time last year.

Still, I felt at "home" there, at my home in Nature.

My memory began to scan the past and all the healing I had received at this very place. Of course, the healing rarely came all at once. But this seemed to be the place where I gained insights that started me on my way to emotional healing.

On the smooth wooden boardwalk over an outlet from the lake, I seated myself and removed my pen and journal from my day pack, just in case I felt inspired to write. Taking a deep breath, I attempted to chase away all thoughts of my life and its many challenges, clearing space for my *present* journey on this retreat.

Now, as I had the time to think about it, I realized that I had been resisting being upset with Mom for years. I guess it was hard to be upset with one's mother, the mother-child relationship being the strongest of ties.

For how could I criticize my mother without feeling wracked with guilt? After all, her body had nourished me for nine months as I grew in her womb. She endured vomiting and backaches, maybe even varicose veins while I was in utero. Then she gave birth.

It felt like sacrilege to criticize Mom. Even that *thought* made me feel like I was committing the most serious sin possible, like my soul was one dark black spot. Still, it was time to examine the full truth about her.

I thought back to what I remembered of her. With her reddish-brown hair and blue eyes, she was attractive and round of face. She stood five feet tall and plump, at least in *my* childhood, though I knew when she married my dad she weighed only ninety-five pounds.

Everyone liked Mom. She was generous, taking cakes to new neighbors who moved in next door, to welcome them, and passing clothes on to them when we outgrew them. Mom was also selfless, almost to a fault, like she didn't feel she *deserved* anything. She wasn't exactly a martyr. Martyrs die for a cause. Mom just felt worthless.

I never felt that she truly loved me as a child or while I was growing up. She provided for me, cared for me, but I always felt that something was missing. Maybe it was a piece of her heart.

A monarch butterfly flitted across in front of me and settled on a yellow water lily floating nearby. As my gaze wandered over the water, I realized that there were many yellow water lilies there. Usually, I had seen only white ones on ponds I'd been near. Butterfly . . . butterfly . . . so beautiful . . . and I began to remember . . .

As a young child, perhaps around the age of five or six, I took to chasing after butterflies as I trailed behind my mother on her daily perusal of her flower gardens. The butterflies were my signal that summer had come once again. What fun!

We'd begin with the peonies that were situated at the far edge of the lawn. The full pink blossoms were heavily scented and deeply colored. They attracted many butterflies and bees. Then we'd move on to the shasta daisies, waving gently in the soft breeze. They stood straight and tall and white as newly fallen snow.

Next came the petite grape hyacinths, colored a deep bluish-purple. They had short thin stalks supporting the tiny bells that smelled so sweet. I'd get right down on the ground to sniff once, twice, three times before we moved on to the next flowers.

These were the multi-colored pansies. Blues, yellows, purples and reds brushed across their brightly painted faces as they gazed upward, always smiling their greeting. I felt cheered by them each day. A warmth seeming to grow inside me as I gazed upon them. I wondered if that was why Mom seemed to hesitate longer there, giving *them* her undivided attention.

We would continue our tour of all the different kinds of plants, purposefully arranged so that the gardens were never without color. She loved all her flowers, and seemed to enjoy this daily check-in, caressing many, assessing the state of health of all with the care she so automatically showed to every plant she grew.

She was gentle yet strong as she moved around the lawn. Some of her flower beds edged the lawn, others filled circles and were situated within its boundaries.

I was surrounded by all the colors of the rainbow and I felt as if I were a part of that rainbow, blending with each hue that I saw. I felt immersed in the beauty of it all. It was a special time of day for me and I looked forward to it. It was a period of time that I spent with my mom when she wasn't involved with the drudgery of housework but with the beauty and simplicity of her gardens.

She was happy there and found fulfillment as her plants responded to her through their bursts of bright colors that they produced for her. A sort of communication was going on there. A bond was formed that could not be severed.

I acquired that precious gift of appreciation of the plant world and the peacefulness abiding there. Mom passed that gift on to me by her example. Together we experienced the refreshment plants provided her. The love and care she showed them initiated their response. I accepted, without question, her gentleness in handling them, aiding in their survival and propagation. I absorbed the gentleness and peacefulness of the garden, of Nature, and a responsibility to care for all aspects throughout their life cycles.

Sometimes, Mom would stop and stay with her plants, pulling up weeds whose presence would soon strangle them. She would extract these weeds with such vigor that it seemed contrary to the gentleness and softness she otherwise exhibited in her garden.

The weeds were the invading enemy and deserved only to be thrust into a weathered bushel basket whose slats were gray and rotting, a testimony to the value of its contents. They were then deposited, with just as much vigor, into the deep gulley that was located behind our house. Such was the life of a weed innocently growing in Mom's garden.

Sorry was the seed of the weed that had been blown there and taken root in the fertile soil of the earth, for its life would be short-lived. And so, even though there was beauty here and some escape from the drudgery, there was still work to be done. Work was, ultimately, inescapable.

As we moved along the gardens, the butterflies and bees would abound. Flying and buzzing could be heard everywhere, but it wasn't noisy. It was the sound of life happening, proceeding onward—germinating . . . sprouting . . . growing . . . reproducing . . . dying. There it was, happening before my eyes and I was a willing witness to it all.

I loved the feeling of the cool, soft green grass beneath my bare feet as I ran, hopped, skipped and jumped along after Mom. Rolling in the grass over and over, I would pause . . . and roll some more, laughing with the feel and comfort of my world . . . there . . . in the garden. But, most of all, I loved the butterflies.

The butterflies I saw there were of many colors. The larger ones were orange and black, some others, that were mainly a lighter orange, were smaller and had different markings. Then there were some which were small, and colored a light blue. Finally, there were the large bright yellow and black ones with some blue on the long hind wings.

I chased them all as I ran among the flowers with bumblebees hiding in the blossoms, as they sipped the nectar from deep within. *Maybe this summer, I'll catch one and keep it all to myself,* I thought.

The closest I came to catching any was when I went for the yellow and black variety. I would stop and watch one alight on a blossom. Then I would slowly try to creep up to it with my hand poised high above, descending lower . . . lower . . . and off it would go to the next blossom. And off I would go. It was great fun and I loved it.

Time went along and then one day, as I was inching my hand toward a butterfly, it seemed to linger there. My hand descended lower . . . lower . . . lower — then I quickly pounced and grabbed, closing my thumb and index finger around the butterfly. Catching a wing, I turned my hand and looked closely as it fluttered in the air, flapping its free wing vigorously.

"Mommy! Mommy! Look what I caught! I caught it! I caught it!" I shouted to my mom, filled with excitement. She was far across the lawn, energetically extracting weeds and didn't look up.

Just then my brother, Buddy, who was home from the service and fifteen years older than I, stuck his head out of the garage and called, "What's going on? What's all the excitement? What do you have there, Debby?"

"I caught it! I caught the butterfly!" I yelled, marveling at the entire event. I couldn't take my eyes off it. "Can I keep it, please?" I pleaded.

"Well, for a little while," he responded, a big smile lighting up his face. "Then we'll have to let it go. It's happier flying amidst the flowers. Let's find a jar to put it in. Better yet, I'll find a jar and you pick a handful of grass."

The butterfly had begun to quiet its movements, having tired itself out. Holding the butterfly in my right hand, I ripped off a bunch of grass with my other hand and ran after him. He picked up a glass jar from the top step near the front door of our house and unscrewed the lid. He held the jar out to me.

"First, the grass," he said, as I slid it inside. "Okay. That's good."

"There's a stick beside your foot," he said. "That needs to go in next for the butterfly to rest on."

The stick was black and the bark was coming off one end. I bent over and picked it up, automatically peeling the bark off as I'd seen my brother do to sticks before.

"It's a little too long. Why don't you break some off?"

I followed his instructions. Of course, I only had one free hand since my other one still gripped one wing of the butterfly. So, squatting down I rested one end of the stick on the ground. Pushing down on the stick with my free hand, I could feel it begin to bend . . . then—Snap! Now there were two sticks. I left one on the ground and carefully slid the other one inside the jar. *I'm so glad that Buddy is here helping me. He knows so much about all kinds of animals and trees.*

"Now—your butterfly. Be careful and gentle with it," he cautioned.

Ever so slowly, I slid my hand into the jar and placed my butterfly inside. Buddy was poised with the lid, carefully placing it on top and then screwing that lid down.

"Now we have to put some holes in the lid," he said. "Let's go look for a nail, maybe in the garage."

So to the garage we went. He handed me the jar to carry as we proceeded on our quest. I couldn't help but stare at my butterfly. It was so beautiful . . . My heart filled with love, warm and radiating, for this captured creature. It slowly opened its wings and closed them again like it was speaking to me through the movement.

"Please don't be scared," I said. "I won't let anyone hurt you. You're perfectly safe."

As Buddy drew closer, he said, "Put the jar down so we can punch some holes in the lid."

As I lowered the jar, I noticed that in one hand he held a rock and in the other I could see a nail peeking out, its point looking strong and sharp.

"Why are you poking holes in the lid?" I asked.

"That's so air can get in and the butterfly can breathe."

My brother placed the point of the nail so it was touching the lid. Then with the rock, he carefully but forcefully tapped the nail until it broke through. He tapped another until it broke through . . . then another. Now we had three holes.

I lifted the jar so I could look right into my butterfly's eyes.

"Can you see me?" I asked. "You're so pretty."

As I shifted the jar back to my right hand, I noticed something yellow on it. *"What is that?"* I brushed my hand back and forth on my pants. Now, I needed to find a place for the jar.

"Where will I keep you?" I asked my butterfly.

He responded by opening and closing his wings.

"And I have to give you a name. How about Hector? I'll keep you in the dining room on the windowsill so you can see the sun when you wake up in the morning. It always shines in there first thing."

And so my days of watching Hector began. I went out to the garden and plucked a pansy blossom and carefully unscrewed the top. I dropped it in beside Hector and stared as my eyes grew in size at the sight. He was looking right at the blossom and began to extend a long tongue-like projection toward the flower. He seemed to uncurl and place it right in the middle of the pansy face. There it remained. *Was he drinking? Wow!*

When he finished, he would curl that tongue right back in and lock it up tight, at least that's what it looked like to me. He would grip the stick with his long black legs and pose for me—so pretty, so beautiful.

I got to keep him for three days. Well, it wasn't quite three days, because on the third day my brother came into my room, first thing after breakfast. "You need to let him go today," he said. "He needs to be free."

Outside I sadly went, onto the patio, carrying the jar with my butterfly inside. There I set it down on the concrete.

"Good-bye, Hector," I said as my eyes began to water. "Thank you for visiting me. I'll see you in the garden, I hope."

I slowly unscrewed the lid and lifted it off the jar, opening it to the blue sky above. But he didn't fly out. I slowly and carefully lifted the stick he was on and pulled it out of the jar, placing it on the wooden railing that encircled the patio.

"You're supposed to fly away now, Hector," I said. "Go. Go."

Still, he didn't fly. I put my finger there instead of the stick. He held on tight to my finger.

"I can feel your feet sticking to me, Hector," I told him. "It kind of tickles."

He opened his wings and closed them again.

"Was that 'Thank you?' Were you saying thank you to me?" I asked him. "Well, you're welcome."

I slowly inched my way around the patio with him clinging to my finger. I felt like we were connected. And so we were. He was counting on me, depending on me. It was up to me. I had captured him and now I was setting him free.

I eased him off of my finger and back onto the white wooden railing where he had rested before on his stick and ventured over to Mom's garden. I left him there to fly away when he was ready, my heart dropping to my toes.

Many times that day, I checked on him to see if he had flown away, but there he remained. Sometimes, it made me happy that he was still there as if he were choosing to stay with me. Other times, I felt saddened because he wasn't among the flowers where I had found him. Sometimes he'd be in a different place on his white wooden perch, but he didn't fly away. When I spoke to him out the window, he'd open and close his wings like we were having a conversation.

That evening, my brother went with me out onto the patio to look more closely at the butterfly. Bending down, he began talking. "What did you name him?" he asked.

"Hector, I replied.

"Hello there, Hector," said my brother. "We're going to see if we can figure out why you aren't flying away. So, I'm just going to nudge you here and see if you'll fly for me."

Hector just wobbled on his long black stick-like legs and then stopped and opened and closed his wings–one . . . two . . . three times.

"That's how he talks. He's telling you 'Thank you'," I said.

"I think he's also trying to show us what his problem is," Buddy said with concern. "Look, here, at his wing." He pointed at a large colorless spot on one wing. "He's lost some of his powder and without that he can't fly—ever."

Quite suddenly, I remembered the yellow powder that I had seen on my fingers when I eased him into the jar. "What color would the powder be?" I asked, holding my breath. *Please don't let it be yellow. Please don't let it be yellow.*

"Yellow," he answered. "The powder he lost was yellow."

The yellow powder I had brushed away onto my pants. It was me. I had done that. The reality of what I had done, what I had caused, hit me hard. *I did that to him when I caught him and now he can't fly—ever.*

The tears began their slow descent down my face. I felt the deepest sadness of all—*I'm to blame for this creature's not being able to fly anymore.* As I stood there, my heart began its downward plunge. "I *didn't know!*" I wanted to scream. "*I didn't know!*"

"Let's put him back in the jar for tonight and think about what we can do about it for tomorrow," he said. "He can stay outside for the afternoon."

"Can we put the powder back on?" I asked.

"No," my brother answered. "That powder is special and it can't be replaced."

My brother knew a lot about the woods and creatures that lived there. If he said it couldn't be fixed, then it couldn't be fixed. Later that day, I lifted Hector onto the edge of a saucer of sugar water that Mom had fixed. He uncurled his tongue and took a long drink.

"I'm so sorry, Hector, that I got your powder on my fingers. I just wanted to watch you up close for a while. I guess I wanted you to be mine. But you don't really belong to me at all. Now you'll *never* be free." I felt like I was withering up inside the way some of mom's flowers did right before they died.

I lifted Hector as he stepped onto my finger and set him down on the concrete patio floor. He began to walk around as I watched.

"What will become of you?" I asked.

"Debby, time for lunch," my mom called.

"I'm going to leave you for a while, Hector. The sun is nice out here. I'll bring you some more sugar water later when I come back out," I told him.

The reality of what I had done and the consequences of my actions caused my heart to plunge again, even deeper. *I did a horrible thing and it's my fault. I'm so, so sorry.*

After lunch, I checked on my butterfly. He was still walking around on the patio. I watched him totter around for a bit, still feeling saddened and sunken within.

Finally, I couldn't watch anymore. My heart just seemed to be crumbling and I couldn't keep from crying when I was with him. He stopped moving and opened and closed his wings as if to say, *"It's okay. These things happen. I'm okay."*

With that, I ran off to the garden of flowers, running

barefoot through the blades of grass, faster and faster until I fell down panting for air. I lay there on the grass, watching all the butterflies flit and fly among the blossoms, all the butterflies . . . but one.

As I lay there, I realized that a truck was turning into our driveway. It was the milkman. As I walked across the lawn, still tired from my run, I noticed Mom opening the door to collect her delivery. The milkman climbed down from his truck with a crate in his hand and walked over to her, climbing our steps.

"Hello, Mrs. Havas," he said in greeting. "It's a real pretty day, today."

"Yes, it is," answered Mom.

"The same order next week?" he asked as he collected our empty milk bottles and gave her the fresh milk.

"Yes, but I'll need more cottage cheese next week. Two containers instead of one and a package of cream cheese, too," she smilingly replied.

"Okay. Got it," the milkman said, writing the order on his pad. He turned to leave, walked down the steps and over to his truck. He swung himself up inside and started the engine. He slowly backed out of our driveway. As he entered the road, he saw me and waved. *Good-bye, Mr. Milkman. I'll see you next week,* I thought as I returned his wave.

Running over to the steps, I began to climb. Mom had already gone inside and closed the screen door. *One step . . . two steps . . . three steps . . .* I was looking down, counting out loud like I always did. Then I saw it. *What was it? There, on the next step. Oh! Not my butterfly!*

I squatted down and looked closer. I could only make out one yellow and black wing, the powder now blowing in the wind around the silent vestige. *How could that happen?*

My heart continued its crumbling dive that it had been on all day and finally smashed, breaking into a million splinters. *Who? How?* The tears poured out of my eyes uncontrollably. *No! No! No! The milkman! It was the milkman who must have stepped on him. He wouldn't see him on a cement step. Butterflies are supposed to be on flowers not resting on cement steps. All butterflies but one . . . one that couldn't fly.*

All I could do was cry. I went inside where I could hear my mom washing up the lunch dishes. The familiar sounds of clean-up were coming from the kitchen.

"My butterfly's dead," I cried as I entered, tears streaming down my face. "The milkman stepped on him."

She turned and glared at me with anger in her eyes, a look of disgust on her face.

"Shame on you, Debby. Shame on you."

She turned back to her dishes.

Suddenly I felt lost and alone. I was left on my own, to bear it all—all those feelings of desolation that overwhelmed and consumed me. I left the kitchen and moved, as if in a daze, to my bedroom. I flopped on my bed and froze. *I really WAS bad, bad, bad . . .*

I learned a grave lesson that day. I had realized that I had the power to destroy, to kill, although I didn't intend to.

If I hadn't wanted to catch that butterfly, he'd still be alive, flying freely from flower to flower. But he wasn't. And I did that. I did that.

As I sat there on the boardwalk my eyes caught movement. Turning my head, I saw a dragonfly skimming across the water near me. As he darted here and there, I found myself beginning to sway with the movement. As I did so, I began to make more sense of my butterfly memory.

The shame that my mom had dealt out was but another layer upon a base of shame that she had already formed within my being. Maybe her mom had dealt with her that way. Shame for what you did, shame for what you desired, shame for what you thought, shame on me.

The butterfly became a metaphor for my spirit, delicate, beautiful and free. I had tried to capture it and put it in a glass cage. It had withered and died. My soul would begin to become caged by people's reactions to me and the messages they sent—*I'm not good*.

Mom's withholding her affection from me would have its effect, causing me to feel driven, and further causing my feeling guilty about relaxing. Her life was drudgery with a capital D. As I got older, Dad's lack of praise or approval would cause my persistent attempts at perfection, something I could never achieve at a level that I could accept. I was on my way . . . but to where?

As I sat beside the water's edge, I searched my memory for other disappointments I'd experienced with my mom. I couldn't think of any time that she came to my defense with my dad, over any issue. Neither did she verbally express any support of me that I can remember. She didn't exhibit any excitement for what I had accomplished that I recall, either. She wasn't a mean person in any way, just not outwardly demonstrative.

When I was young it was difficult to know what she thought about anything except when I stepped over an invisible line and entered the world of *shame*. That was *very* evident as the feeling of being lost and alone descended and the sense grew that I was *bad . . . bad . . . bad*. I was a bad person, again.

10

JUST EMPTY

Still sitting by the water, I noticed a butterfly moving among the wildflowers growing near the boardwalk. It seemed so free, flitting from blossom to blossom as I watched.

My spirit *yearns to be free*, I thought. *But how am I to get there?*

I felt so enclosed, restricted. *Am I doing it to myself? Is it the lack of forgiveness that is doing it?*

"Okay, Mom," I said out loud, "I guess I need to forgive you, too, besides Dad. Just please don't pass away until I work through this. Please. I don't want to carry this, too. What more do I need to remember? What more do I need to be aware of, to forgive you?"

I began realizing now how much *Mom* had affected me over the years. I always felt that it was *Dad* whom I had grown to hate. He was outwardly bitter, angry and mean. Yet, I really had been resisting coming to terms with the effects *Mom* had on me.

I didn't *hate* her. I never had. I'd seen her as a victim of Dad's anger and meanness. But she also had a hand in making me feel worthless. Her words rang through my head. *Shame on you!*

My mind began to search my high school years. Another set of memories returned. The deep hurt came crashing down, crushing me until I felt like my heart was being ripped out. *Was I strong enough to face it?*

I entered junior high school in an anxious yet excited mode. Things were so different. We had to carry our books as we changed classes and had only three minutes to maneuver to our next one. My heart was racing, trying to get there in time.

Beyond these worries was a greater one. How would I fit in? Would the others like me? As I adjusted to the routine, I became more relaxed. Slowly I felt like I was finding my niche.

My greatest joy was physical education class. I knew I was in pretty good shape. What would the other girls think? Would I impress them? Maybe I'd even become popular.

Deep beneath the surface, though, an uneasy truth was forming. I would not really ever fit in, anywhere. I was not good enough. But that sense was not fully formed or solid yet. There was a chance I might do something that would make me stand out and be worthy of being liked.

What made the class great, besides my own personal hopes, was that I really liked the teacher. She was twenty-six years old and had the greatest smile. It warmed me each time I saw her. Her twinkling eyes threw a wink my way each time we had contact. That wink made me feel reassured. It said, "I like you. You're doing fine. I approve." Her nose was a bit crooked, probably from a sports injury, but I didn't care. Even if I was having a stressful day, it cheered me up to see her.

At one point, my teacher was required to give us the New York State Physical Fitness Tests. In the end, my scores amazed both of us. I ranked in the highest percentile possible. She even had me repeat the agility and endurance parts of the test with her doing the counting, instead of my partner. The result was the same. I'd set the school record for the endurance challenge.

"You did a great job, Debby! Well done!" she exclaimed.

I was stunned. I drank in her words of praise the way dry roots would drink in a downpour. Praise was something I had never experienced before. I seemed to have above average physical abilities. I had also excelled in the speed and strength tests that comprised the rest of the physical evaluation.

For a moment I actually felt proud of myself, and then embarrassment descended. My family would not be proud. I had been taught not to feel pride. Suddenly, I felt ashamed that I'd felt that pride. Now I was caught in a quandary. It felt good to feel proud of myself. How could something that was so bad feel this good?

When we began our stunts and tumbling unit, I could do no wrong. My sense of balance was great and my coordination seemed likewise. As a small gal, I was always the top of the pyramids that we built. My teacher used me to demonstrate any stunts she felt needed illustration. It made me feel special and again I could feel that pride creeping in. I would try to shove it back down from whence it came—down deep in my gut. Sometimes I was successful ridding myself of pride and sometimes I wasn't.

When I wasn't, I would experience a too-familiar feeling. Shame, that sense of defectiveness, would bring me down and I would feel badly about the person I was. Why could I not stop my sense of pride from overcoming my guardedness?

Yet, time and again, that bubbling up of positive emotion would flood my whole being, causing me to smile and laugh. Then I'd feel an even deeper sense of shame.

My love for tumbling in my junior high years expanded to gymnastics in high school. Fortunately, I had the same teacher as before, since we lived in a very small school district. This was great! My spirit soared! I hoped that I could become a worthwhile person, that someone would see something good about me or about what I did.

In preparation for the gymnastics unit, the Phys. Ed. teacher had ordered some new equipment. In class we rotated to each piece, old and new. There were rings, parallel bars, the horse, ropes, trampoline, mats, uneven parallel bars and the balance beam. After experiencing all, I was drawn to the balance beam, encouraged by my teacher.

"You have a great sense of balance, Debby. Your movements just seem to flow," she told me.

There was my enemy again—that feeling of pride, the pride my parents had so carefully sought to rid me of by not praising anything I did.

We began to work ninth period and after school during our intramural time. There was an invitational gymnastics meet scheduled in a city some distance away. She told us that some of us were going to it. And I was going!

My role was to represent our school on the balance beam. I'd created my own routine which included the required moves set by the host school.

The routine I created included two advanced moves which were jumps high into the air, a squat jump and a hesitation jump. The routine was to include three passes on the four inch wide beam, which was four feet off the ground. I was thrilled. I couldn't believe I was part of the team. If only I could keep from thinking too much of myself. I hated it when others bragged about themselves, whether it was over their grades, what they did or what they had. I didn't want to become like that.

Inside, I felt quite confused, almost like a war was going on. On the one hand, I wanted to be liked. I wanted to do well. On the other hand, if I did accomplish something good, I would not speak of it. That would be bragging.

My parents made it clear that bragging was bad. Even to think *well* of myself was pride. Pride was even worse. Pride was to be squelched. People who did well, and knew it, and spoke of it, and felt good about it; they were prideful. A prideful person was not to be praised. If someone were to praise you for anything, your only response should be something like, "Oh no, not me. I'm not really *that* good. There's so much I have to work on still."

I did not see it at the time, but I was already programmed to minimize what was good about myself.

The flaws, however, were numerous and therefore deserved my concentrated focus. It was almost as if I had to feel badly about myself in order to feel good about myself.

Watching people arrive at church each Sunday was an example. We always selected a pew that was in the middle of the congregation, not too far back and certainly not too far forward. We would watch the wealthy people march up to the front rows, proudly displaying their matching, elegant clothing. They carried themselves upright, focusing ahead. They knew where they were going. They even *looked* confident. My parents called them "big shots" with disgusted tones in their voices. I, therefore, concluded that it was *bad* to be proud and confident and well-dressed, at least in my parents' eyes.

There was probably some jealousy there or at least an assumption that they had not come by that status honestly or deservedly and that they were flaunting it. At the impressionable age I was, their attitude spoke as loudly as though they were shouting at me. It is *bad* to be proud, confident and well-dressed, but you will be clean! That is the attitude I absorbed.

Mom and Dad were not confident people. Maybe their parents hadn't been either. Respect was valued, as was cleanliness. The fact that they were from immigrant families might have caused them to assume that they were not as *good* as the general population. That false assumption might also have affected their attitudes. And, of course, their economic level was lower than most.

This attitude attached itself to me like a virus and I began to judge my classmates, especially those from well to do families, in the same light. I avoided contact with them and developed jealousies of their popularity and possessions.

I was never rude to them and certainly didn't plot against them, but I did think that they were better than I was. This attitude didn't do much for my own self-image or for my self-worth which I was struggling with at the time and would for years to come.

The day of the competition, we changed into our leotards and proceeded into the gym. Some of the other schools were practicing.

I was in awe of all the equipment and the immense size of

the gym itself. Never having been to a city school before, I was nervous.

I made my way to a place on the floor near the balance beams, where I sat down to watch others practice, awaiting my turn. It was all truly amazing. I felt excited and scared at the same time. My heart felt like it was in a vice. *I had to get through this. I had to do well for my school, my teacher and myself.*

Right in front of me, there was a girl doing a very advanced move called a front walkover. I swallowed hard. I'd only seen a picture of that before. *Oh my goodness! She was certainly going to place first!*

As I watched her, her every move on the beam spoke of her confidence in herself. She was in control. It was so obvious. I didn't feel the kind of confidence she exuded, not at all.

What am I doing here? I felt my heart drop in my chest. My routine seemed so simple in comparison, yet I was representing our school.

My heart began racing and I noticed a clammy feeling in my hands. My muscles had tightened and my stomach felt as if it were tied up in a knot.

My gym teacher came over to me, and in the encouraging way she always had toward me, stopped my emotional descent.

"You can do this, Debby. I know you can. Just do your best," she told me.

There it was. No high expectations, just assurance and encouragement. With that wink of her eye, I felt my nervousness melt away. That's what I loved about her. She cared enough to give me her time and presence and the effect was like a pure miracle every time. It was as if she knew what I needed.

The words themselves were not as important as the person she was and the spirit in which she spoke. She was kind, caring, empowering. It worked. She could make my heart soar just by smiling at me because, I realized, she had confidence in me. That was it! I just had to stay on that beam for me, or for her. Maybe it was for me *AND* for her.

With practice time over, I took my designated place and sat down. I decided not to watch the other competitors. I didn't want to see how well they did. My confidence, which had been given a boost by my teacher, was slipping the longer I sat there. Time dragged on.

Then, all at once someone was announcing my name. *Please help me to do the best I can.* That was always my prayer before any exam I took. Repeating it now seemed an automatic act. I stood and walked over to the place from which I would mount the beam. I looked over at the head judge, awaiting her nod.

I kept trying to ease my racing heart, taking some deep breaths. I closed my eyes for a second. When I opened them, I was looking at the head judge as she began to nod. I smiled. It was time, *my* time.

As I mounted the beam with a straddle mount, my legs split wide and my grip was solid, my finger muscles contracting on the beam to hold me on. *Here I go.*

I began to perform my balances, turns, scales and jumps which allowed me to complete two of the three passes of the beam. I knew I was doing well. *I feel so good.*

By now I wasn't even thinking. All I could do was visualize my next moves and deliver. *I've got this,* I told myself. *Now for my final pass. Here it goes.*

I moved into a forward shoulder roll with all the grace I could muster. Rising, I took some quick steps to the end, kicking up into a cartwheel dismount, landing evenly balanced.

It was over. Relief flooded my body. All that work, all those hours . . . and I hadn't fallen off! But what did the judges think of my routine?

My breathing returned to normal and my whole body relaxed. As time moved forward, I again began to hold my breath. I made my way to where the other girls were waiting for their respective turns at each of the stations.

"You looked great!" "Good job." "Well done."

From somewhere down inside me, a thick layer of resistance appeared. I would not let these remarks go to my head. But I *wanted* to feel good about myself. *No.* The resistance struggled against my desire to be liked, even admired.

Looking across the gymnasium, I could see the judges conferring. *What about? What did they think of me?*

It was time for the next competitor . . . the girl with all her confidence, her advanced moves, and her beautiful walkover. She mounted and did well, moving with confidence and poise.

Now for the walkover. Stepping into the move . . . she fell off the beam! That meant a one point deduction from her score right away. She got up and hopped right back on the beam and prepared again. Now, there she goes, but again she fell off.

Was this really happening? She'd done the move so many times during practice. She didn't give the impression of being at all nervous *then*, but clearly she was now. She really was quite shaken.

She must be feeling terrible.

My heart went out to her. The third attempt, a failure, was her demise. Three points had already been deducted from her score. She got back on, and I could see her demeanor had changed. She seemed defeated. That was when I realized:

I know what that feels like, to feel badly about yourself, like you're nothing but a failure.

The competition had ended. Place finishes on each piece of equipment were announced. My name was called.

Could it be? Me? Yes!

I was awarded the blue ribbon for first place. The feeling that was being crushed down inside me, of wanting to do well; no, of wanting to do great, and be rewarded for all my hard work—that feeling surged through my whole body.

The excitement bubbled up from the depths of my being, rising and finally bursting at the surface. I allowed it to remain there. I basked in it. My face beamed with joy and pride at my accomplishment.

"Great job, Debby! Great job! You did it. I'm proud of you," my teacher said, smiling broadly, her eyes twinkling. And then that *wink*. There it was.

I was bursting. My heart was about to explode, I was so filled with joy. I smiled. I laughed. I cried. I was *so* happy.

The bus ride home went quickly with all the girls sharing their experiences, their evaluations of the other competitors, even comments about the judges. I shared some but mostly I listened.

I had worked hard and put in so many hours practicing. It had, indeed, paid off. I felt so good . . . I couldn't wait to tell my mom.

My teacher gave me a ride home. I lived about a mile from her house, out in the country. That's how I got home from most athletic events. I could depend on her or my brother for transportation. My dad wouldn't provide any. He was indifferent to my participating in sports at all.

Once inside the door, I ran into my mom and dad's bedroom where I found my mom. She was in there ironing, as usual.

"I got first place!" I yelled excitedly, displaying my blue ribbon. A feeling of elation was exploding through all my muscles, like popcorn kernels of joy.

My mother didn't even look up. She kept running the iron over the white bed sheets spread out on the ironing board. When she spoke, her voice held a tone of disgust.

"Where's *that* going to get you?"

I froze.

Then in an instant, my heart fell. Turning, my chest tightening, I walked out the door and down the hall into my bedroom. Closing the door, I flopped onto my bed as a great layer of stone dropped down on me.

I lay on the bedspread for hours, sobbing, wrenching in pain and also despair. *Why wasn't anything I ever accomplished good enough to reward me with even the smallest remark of kindness or praise? Why weren't the things I liked important? I had tried so hard. What could be better than first place? What could I do? How could I top that?*

I felt betrayed by my own mother. *Wasn't she supposed to be excited that I had won? Wasn't she? She was my mother!*

A sense that I was not worth anyone's time or attention settled in on me. What I felt was not the betrayal I'd experienced when a confidante revealed a secret or when someone told a lie about me. That hurt but this was much deeper.

The betrayal I now experienced came from the sudden, total loss of trust in one of the most important people in my life.

There was another feeling, layered on top of that. From then on, the sense of insecurity I'd felt about myself deepened. I didn't feel safe in the world or even in my own home, and it wasn't a new feeling. After all, I'd been soaring higher than I'd ever been before and got hit by a bolt of lightning that leveled me to the ground. I knew then that at any moment I might say or do something that was important to me and again be struck down.

Now, who could I share my joys and sorrows with? Not my mother.

It cut deeply, descending into the dark recesses of who I was growing up to be and lingered there, festering until it popped up again and again as I proceeded on my journey. Once more, probably at the worst moment, the message had come to me loud and strong.

You are not worthy of my support, maybe not even of my love.

It had taken many years before I was ready to begin to recognize the source of my feelings of unworthiness. In time, this one event sank into the background of life's landscape. Still, its traumatic impact was long-lasting, not just because of the words which were spoken, but also because the person who spoke them had held a place of supreme importance to me.

Her tone of voice had expressed total disgust. It told me that my joys, desires and excitement were disgusting to her.

Maybe I *am disgusting to Mom, too—the very person that I am.*

My heart had curled up within me that day. Dreams and

aspirations had crumbled and died. I had felt only constriction, a pulling down and a withdrawing into myself of all that I was.

As I said, life and events moved on. The scar tissue on my soul was forgotten. But it was not without its own power. It became a burden that I would carry for a long, long time.

That was my mom. That was our relationship. I didn't feel that her treatment of me was justified. I wanted to understand why she acted that way toward me. She certainly didn't act the same way toward my other three siblings, at least not that I noticed.

Then I remembered the way things were when I was born—how my life began and how hers had been at the time. I remembered the conditions she had to live with and the lack of love and support from my dad that she had to contend with.

I began to see it all—how it wasn't *me* or that she didn't *love* me. She had just burned out from caring for children and the task of living. There wasn't anything left. She was empty and I absorbed that emptiness. I felt it . . . I carried it . . . and it grew in me like an infection.

Mom had not *intended* to be mean or to seem uncaring toward me. Being mean just wasn't in her makeup. She was just empty.

I knew that she grew to love me and I always loved her. I tried to show her by picking flowers for her and surprising her with little gifts that I would make. I so enjoyed giving them to her just to see her smile. She didn't smile or laugh all that much.

In my adult years, however, her comment on my little surprises that I would give her was always the same.

"Oh, you shouldn't have done that," she would say.

That would really take all the fun out of the gift giving for me. The first time it happened, I really felt quite hurt, like I was a little girl again and I'd done something wrong. Then I realized what she was feeling. She was reacting that way because she felt that she didn't *deserve* any gifts.

I persisted anyway in my gift giving because I *wanted* to do that. I still had fun planning what I would make for her the next time I saw her. Over time, I began to disregard her reaction, but it was still somewhat depressing. It had never changed for either of us all these years.

When we would meet, we didn't talk about our struggles nor did Mom share much of her history with me. I never even told her of my diagnosis. We'd talk about my girls, my projects, the weather and my siblings. We never touched on the personal or how we felt about anything.

We missed out on a lot in our relationship. There was a sadness about that, but I did understand after spending time thinking and remembering. There was not much more that we could do about the past but forgive it. There was no harsh intention ever meant on her part.

She was just empty.

FORGIVENESS

As my retreat continued, I knew I had gained more of an understanding of my mom, which was a pleasant surprise. But what about Dad?

I awakened in my room. A new day was dawning. I turned my head to look at the plant I'd brought along to my retreat this year. It stood there, on my desk by the window, lush, vibrant, *alive*. It reminded me of the new life awaiting me that comes after forgiveness arrives, and I began to think about forgiveness.

Forgiving Mom involved realizing what her life was like at the time I was born and even before I was born. As I lay there, I remembered what a wise person once told me.

"People try to do the best they can at the time," she said.

I thought of my mom again and the baggage she had probably carried from her own upbringing, all the disappointments that life had allowed her to encounter. Once I had become privy to some of them, I thought about how *I* might have responded under similar circumstances. I realized that I probably would have responded very similarly, which allowed a particular empathy to awaken in me.

I had begun to understand not only *why* she reacted as she did but *how* that reaction had affected her child, *me*. Seeing the whole picture had really opened my eyes, not only to *her* but to how *many* people reacted to situations, maybe even *why* they did so.

Forgiveness was the next step. It was certainly made easier through understanding the intentions and motivations behind Mom's behavior. Once I had understood, I could begin to forgive her. That's what was happening now, each day. I felt a warmth bubbling up inside. That warmth I identified as the power of forgiveness. My inability to forgive her all these years had made me a much unhappier person. I now felt freer, as if a great burden had been lifted off my heart.

I knew the greatest challenge was yet to come—that of forgiving my dad.

Still, I was hopeful. If it could happen with my mom, it might be possible with Dad, too. I thought it might be more difficult with him, though. For one thing, he was no longer alive. I couldn't give him a loving hug after I'd come through my struggle. No, that was going to be much more difficult.

I couldn't remember *ever* loving my father. I grew to *hate* my father. And hatred affects both parties involved. It slowly eats away like a cancer but it's a cancer of the soul. It affects how we look at things, how we look at other people and how we respond to situations. It affects the opinions we form, the prejudices we develop and the expectations we place on others and on ourselves. In the case of hating a parent, it affects the choices we make for a lifetime partner. Some women select a mate who is similar to their own dads, whom they love and respect. Others, who don't admire their dads, choose someone they feel is entirely different. I fell into the former category.

I found someone who wasn't anything like my dad, or so I thought. My dad was dark complexioned, broad and tall, with brown eyes. I chose someone who was shorter, medium built, fair-skinned and blue-eyed. As time went on, however, I began to recognize similar qualities. Though they didn't look at all alike physically, both were uncomfortable expressing affection or talking about feelings. That was my realm of existence.

I wonder if I can at least come to understand him. The only cure for the burden I carry is forgiveness.

Armed with my pen, journal and a pocket full of tissues, I once again took the woodland path to the smooth wooden boardwalk by the lake. There I sat and gazed around me, ridding myself of cares and worries. I opened myself up to a new viewpoint. I didn't want any emotion to be blocking the possibility of my healing.

My early memory of my dad was his coming home after working away as a builder of bridges. He would bring me a rubber cowboy on his horse or an Indian. (Westerns were popular at that time on television.) I grew a collection of them and would spend hours playing with them under the dining room table. Sometimes he would bring me a box of lollipops. However, there would be neither hug nor kiss nor swoop up into his arms when he arrived.

He was not affectionately demonstrative. He also didn't believe in giving gifts on birthdays or Christmas. Instead, my brother and mother would come through on my birthday with a gift from the two of them. When my two sisters began working away from home, they would send something, also. I didn't need much. It was the *remembering* that really counted to me.

Is that why, in my adult life, I make a point of remembering birthdays, even of casual friends I have made? I have realized that they are quite surprised when I do, and don't necessarily reciprocate on *my* birthday. It seems they have many people who remember them and many gifts are received. I realize that it's much more important to *me* and I believe there's a very good reason. There is an emptiness that needs to be refilled each birthday, an assurance that I am of value, at least to some. And many people don't *need* that. Remembering my day says to me, "You matter."

Is that why I have to celebrate a birthday on the *exact* date? It's almost like I'm trying to make up for the birthday parties I never had or even the lack of celebration at my *own* birth. *Can I ever make up for all of that?* I wonder . . .

Thinking back, Mom would always make me a Delmonico steak on my birthday and it was *only* for me. The family didn't join me in my special entrée, but we all indulged in the chocolate cake with chocolate icing that she would bake.

I certainly remembered my birthday gift. It was very special when you only got *one* on that day. Again, there was something special about getting your gift *on* your birth date. It didn't seem to matter much to other people if a gift came on their birthday or not or even if their birthday was celebrated on that or another day.

It did to me.

Forgiveness, how elusive you are,
And what do you require of me?
I recognize the need for you,
The way I do not see.

An open heart I bring to you,
This empty hole is still to be,
Rid me of my brokenness,
Let me feel whole and free.

As I sat there by the water's edge, I visualized my dad as I remember him when I was a child.

My dad had dark hair and brown eyes. His skin was always dark, almost black due to his exposure to the sun while working on the bridges he was employed to build. He was really wide, with shoulders as big as a house. At least that's how they seemed to me as a child. He had a large mole on his lower chest. It looked to me like a big black wart. It popped right out! Dad was very good at his construction trade and could figure measurements in his head; pretty good for having only an eighth grade education.

I also learned that he had played drums in a band to earn money when he was a young man, though I never witnessed him tapping out even a rhythm in my years at home. He had been directed to quit school in order to earn a wage, thereby contributing to the support of the family which included two brothers at the time. They eventually ended up doing very well for themselves financially.

On the contrary, Dad struggled with finding work all his life.

I never knew my uncles on my dad's side of the family. There was nothing but hard feelings there. I felt much bitterness in the room when their names were brought up. So, Dad had family he wasn't close to, didn't speak with and wasn't a part of anymore. I wonder whether I absorbed some of that sense of absence also, my desire to belong being so intense.

I remember the yelling that seemed to dominate his time at home and Mom crying, the topic being mostly about money. He even raged about the brand of potato chips that she had bought. It was not a pleasant atmosphere when Dad was home. I was glad to see him leave each week.

The years of his being on unemployment came. The frequency of the yelling episodes increased. We went on the Surplus Foods Program and Mom worked wonders. Obviously, money became even tighter than before.

My hatred for my father grew. He was not a pleasant man. He was not a happy man. He was an embittered man.

As I became an adult, I became more aware of some of his demons, money being one of them. I realize now how I have absorbed many of his money issues without even knowing it.

There didn't ever seem to be enough money when I was young, so I became a saver. Saving is a positive practice, but there was an intensity within me that I always *had* to save. The item should be on sale for me to purchase it. I remember passing up many an item, especially clothes and food, if it wasn't on sale.

I remember being agitated with myself if I bought gas at one station and saw that a mile down the road, it was $ .03 cheaper

per gallon. Somehow, I had messed up. That was how it made me feel inside. That was from my dad.

What do I remember from my childhood that caused me great pain? I know I have to go back there . . . to my transparent yellow plastic piggy bank. I'm thinking I was maybe five or six at the time.

Conversation quieted as we finished our supper. Mom had made her Hungarian specialty, stuffed cabbage, which we all loved—especially me. The meal had culminated with her famed chocolate cake smothered in chocolate icing. Dishes had been collected and tea served. My dad, who was not a tea drinker, preferred coffee. All throughout the meal I had been wondering, excitedly anticipating what had become a Friday evening routine for us, for Dad and me.

Will he remember? Oh, I hope so... When is he going to call me to come?

Then, the words that I had been anxiously awaiting came. "Debby, come over here." That was my dad, speaking directly to me!

I climbed out of my chair and scurried to the end of the blue-enameled, metal-topped table where Dad always sat to eat his meals when he was at home. As soon as I got there, he stood up at his place and emptied his pockets, the change striking the table. First one pocket and then the other lost its contents.

"Let's find all the nickels," he would say, as we both separated them out from all the other change. "How many do we have?" he next would ask.

Together, we would begin to count out loud as many nickels as we could find, "One . . . two . . . three . . . four . . . "

When we were finished, he'd place one hand at the edge of the table, palm up, and with the sweeping movements of the other hand, all the nickels would end up in his palm. Sometimes only one sweep was required and at other times, it would take more, depending on how many nickels there were.

Next he would get up from the table and proceed down the long hallway to his bedroom, nickels in hand, with me following. The first time we had done this, I wondered where the nickels would end up. Now I knew.

As we entered the bedroom, he moved over to his dresser. There, high up on the top, a transparent, yellow plastic pig was standing, a token for opening an account at the local bank. Dad would transfer the nickels, one by one, placing them into the slot that was cut in the top of the plastic pig.

Again we would count together, "One . . . two . . . three . . . four . . . " as each coin fell and clunked into the others already congregating there. Each week I would watch the nickels fill to a higher level.

Only Dad would drop in the nickels. Only Dad would touch the transparent yellow plastic pig.

I would go to sleep peacefully at night, knowing that we were feeding that pig and wondering what would happen when it was finally filled. *Would it be used to buy something for ME? After all, it was something Dad and I were doing together, so it must be for ME. I wonder what the prize at the end of this long ritual will be.*

Dad would leave for the following week of work on Monday morning, and I would keep an eye on that pig, checking to see where the level stayed. At times, I would run into that back room with a great deal of gusto, and at other times I would tip-toe, making scarcely a sound.

Often I would check on that pig after breakfast, sometimes after lunch and *always* after supper. I felt that I had a responsibility to keep an eye on things until another week had gone by and Dad and I went into the bedroom to deposit the nickels again. So, week by week, the pig would be fed. And I watched the level get higher . . . and higher . . . and higher.

Finally, one Friday came and we took our last contribution of nickels in to the bedroom. Dad dropped them in, "One . . . two . . . three . . . four . . ." as we counted again out loud. *Is there room for one more?* I wondered. *We had five nickels this time. Will the last one fit?*

Dad took hold of the pig with one hand and shook it. I watched as the nickels shifted, some resisting the movement. Others moved quite easily, making enough room for that very last nickel. Then Dad held our fifth nickel and squeezed it in.

"There," he said. "It's full." With that, he left the room.

"It's full! It's full!" I shouted, jumping up and down, the excitement gushing through my body like a dam that had broken. I bounced down the hallway to my bedroom, still jumping as I entered. *This is so great! So great! I wonder what I'll get!*

Monday morning, Dad left for his week of work again. As soon as I finished my breakfast, I ran into his bedroom. I stopped in front of his tall dresser, slowly raising my eyes up to that pig, hope and excitement fighting for possession of my soul.

But something was wrong. My pig looked different. I quietly crept closer. I didn't understand. I couldn't believe my eyes.

I can see right through him. How can that be? Where did all the nickels go?

And then realization struck. "No! No!" I cried. "My pig is empty!" Tears began to trickle down my cheeks. I stood on my tiptoes and grabbed onto the wooden dresser handles, boosting me up a little higher still. There I saw it. It was not only empty but it was cracked up where the slot was located, that same slot that Dad had used to drop in the nickels all those weeks. *Someone had broken into that piggy bank and stolen the money. I was bewildered. Who would do that?*

I stood there aghast, tears still rolling down my cheeks. Then it hit me. *Dad. It was Dad. Dad broke into the piggy bank and stole the money.* That special time we had spent together now lost all its meaning, all its specialness.

I never asked anyone *what* had happened or *why* it had happened and no one ever explained anything about it to me. No one ever said anything at all, and I knew better than to ask. What I had seen as a gift—the time together, the excitement, the anticipation of something purchased for *me* with the money, it had all been taken away from me, *stolen from me by my own father.*

Something vital drained out of me a bit that day. I felt wiped out. Depleted.

Later I would come to understand: the excitement that had been building inside me all those weeks was the physical expression of a life force and it had been taken from me by my parent. I took that to mean that anyone could break in and take something from me at any time. That action said to me, "You don't really need this." That belief became incorporated into my being and would dictate my choices for years to come.

As I thought back on it later, I couldn't remember Dad ever telling me that we were saving the nickels especially for me. I, as a young child, had assumed it from the special ritual we had together.

The effect was profound on me even as an adult. I not only became a saver of money, which can be a positive thing, but another lesson had been impressed on me. I could not use any of it on *myself* unless I deemed it absolutely necessary. I would sacrifice and do without so I could save some. I was *compelled* to save.

As an adult, I saved more glass jars than I would ever need, under the guise of "Maybe I will need it someday." I had more boxes than I would ever use for gifts. I even saved clothes that were tattered and worn out.

The introduction of recycling has been a blessing, for it has allowed me to transition. I was not throwing away. The jar, the box could eventually be reused by others even in an altered state. That resulted in allowing me to feel like I was benefitting others, as well as my children, my grandchildren and planet earth, too.

It was the feeling deep inside *of being without* that wasn't pleasant, of needing something to insure that I wasn't empty, as empty as the transparent yellow plastic pig. It was a form of protection of the self, for I had felt violated at a very young age.

"Dad, *you* did that to me," I said aloud as the tears poured from my eyes. The emptiness I was feeling was so vacant. Like there was nothing inside of me at all—no *me*.

Where I was sitting, at the lake's edge on the smooth wooden boardwalk, I noticed beneath me a small waterfall. The water rushed over the rocks, dropping below on its way to who knows where. It was always changing, like life, like me.

With each awareness and experience, I *also* experienced change. Nature was always changing. Maybe that was why I did not tire of walking the same path in the woods, day after day. I knew that it would never be the exact same experience.

Then why was I comfortable with routines and schedules? It was like I had a need for constancy, for sameness. Was it because there was a security about having a schedule? Was I that insecure? Had it all begun with my transparent yellow plastic pig? Certainly it was a topic to dwell on another day.

I arose and prepared to leave, collecting my belongings and taking a last look at the falls.

"It doesn't matter where you are going, does it," I said aloud, staring at the fish swimming alongside the boardwalk, "as long as you reach your final destination. And you don't worry about how you're going to get there. Maybe that's a good lesson for *me*."

With that final thought, I proceeded back to the retreat house, feeling like *I* did not have to know where I was going either, as long as I reached *my* final destination.

12

A LETTER TO DAD

I was at the falls again the following day. My spiritual director had instructed me to write a letter to my dad, telling him of the hurts I remembered and how they had made me feel. And so, I began. It all seemed to flow out of me like the water rushing over the falls beneath.

June 26

Dear Dad,

There was never a closeness between us. The only time I remember sitting on your lap as a child was to put money in the collection basket at church. That moment was soon over. That was the only holding I remember.

As far as birthdays, I'd get one present from Mom and Buddy, but why didn't you give me a present or say Happy Birthday to me? That made me feel like I didn't deserve it, that there was something wrong with me.

The night Mom and you had the argument over my math average of 75 on my report card; I was so scared as I lay in my bed. That's when I began to put distance between us. I withdrew within myself and the block wall began to rise between us. It didn't seem to matter to you that I had tried. I was no longer accepted, no longer as smart as my sister, Bonita.

In math class, when I was called up to the board to do a problem, I would freeze up and begin to cry. Did you know that?

Mom and you would have so many arguments and I would experience so much fear. The fear grew into hatred. I lived for school or being in the woods. The house was not a pleasant place with you there.

You were out of work a lot and there were more arguments. You hated your son; that was obvious. You threw a dish of tuna fish across the kitchen, smashing it against the cupboard. Mom sat across from me with a look of horror on her face. Then you ordered him out of the house with a shotgun, he who came to my games (when I was a cheerleader) and transported me so I could be in after-school activities.

I loved him. You hated him. I hated you more.

You never accepted me for who I was and I never got to know who you were.

The tears began to flow . . . the pain was so deep. The sadness tore at my heart.

Neighbors no longer visited. No laughter, no smiles. You began visiting the local bar each day and wasting money while Mom tried to hold it together on so little.

You made Mom return the potato chips to the shelf because they cost $.10 more than another brand.

The day the (Carpenter's) Union called you to work and you crawled to the phone because you were so drunk . . . that made me feel sick inside, humiliated. I lost all respect for you that night. You turned my stomach (as I watched you crawling down the hallway). There was a dying sensation inside me, like I was withering on the vine. Mom and you were the vine, my vine, and I was the fruit, shriveling, shrinking inside, and powerless to affect the situation.

I paused in my writing and stared across the lake. I watched the ripples on the water like lifelines, radiating outward in concentric circles. I watched as they disappeared, never to know their effect.

As I had lost respect for my parent, the pain had cut deep to my core and destroyed much of my own self-respect. Respect was vital to my own emotional health, for if I did not respect myself, how could my ripples travel outward? What could their effect be, if anything?

> *"You were supposed to be my model, Dad, my protector and defender,"* I said aloud as I wrote. *"Instead you became my destroyer, of much of what was good within me. It was as if I'd been sentenced to a slow death."*
>
> *Bud lost respect for you, too. Why do you think he loved Mom so much and her, him? He saw what you were putting her through and what you were denying her because of your ego and pride. You would never ask for help, would you? Not then . . . the big shot Havases.*
>
> *Bud was a good son and he still is. He did things for Mom to make her life easier. You resented all that and your jealousy increased. I used to hear you yell and argue that she (Mom) loved him more than you.*
>
> *Then another argument—"How do I know she's even mine?" Dad yelled.*
>
> *"Sh-h-h, Steve, she'll hear you," Mom replied with anguish in her voice.*
>
> *I heard and prayed that I wasn't yours. I didn't want to be your child. I felt no shame (at the thought) that Mom might have done such a thing.*
>
> *In college you gave me a check for dorm costs. I gave it back to you.*
>
> *"I don't want your money or need your money," I told you.*

*I didn't want anything from you, for what I
really needed, you could never give.*

Suddenly I stopped writing, struck with a scene from my
past invading my present moment, demanding my attention. I
had been planning my wedding.

The wedding plans had been made. We were to be married
in mid-August, a few weeks before the start of school, since I
had my teaching position to resume. My fiancée was searching
for a teaching position, with applications out to the five districts
under fifty miles away from mine.

There were no openings in my district for him to fill.

Something will appear. I know it will. That's what we thought.

The next step was to meet with my parents to tell them the
final plan. I met this requirement with a great deal of dread. It
meant speaking directly with them. I hadn't spoken much to my
dad over the years, nor had he initiated conversation with me.
We were at a stalemate.

Both my mom and dad had met Tom before and knew
that he was a presence in my life. What I wanted had never
been a high priority for them, and I had some different ideas
for my wedding ceremony, nontraditional at that time. My
two sisters and my brother had all opted for traditional cer-
emonies. Tom opted not to be present at all for the parental
meeting, and so it was up to me to meet with my parents
alone.

I had become quite active in the parish in my little town
where I was teaching. The pastor was young and enthusiastic.

I volunteered to help him with the CYO, having all of the girls in my physical education classes already.

It was fun for us all. He was a great asset for the youth, open to their thoughts and ideas, a good listener. So here is where I wanted to have my ceremony, instead of in my home parish where I didn't have any close ties or experience any warm, cozy feelings, ever.

I also had some other unique ideas. I wanted the song, "I Believe", sung before I walked down the aisle. That was one beautiful song which spoke volumes to me. I wanted, "We've Only Just Begun", sung after the wedding vows were exchanged. Three of my students were to be my chorus and guitarist throughout the ceremony.

I wished to have the wild daisies of the field for my wedding bouquet. They were simple, delicate, and of the earth I loved so much, that I had bonded with in my early years as my refuge and respite. They needed to be with me at this time as I began yet another phase of my journey.

We would tent on Raquette Lake, in the Adirondack Mountains of New York State, for our honeymoon, since that is where we had met, both of us on the work-study program offered by our college. All of these things were different from the norm at that time.

I had saved my money from teaching since, other than food and rent, I didn't have many expenses.

I didn't own a car. I rented a simple apartment over a garage a few doors down from the school building in which I taught.

My National Defense Student Loan didn't have to be paid off immediately. If I could teach for five years in a public school,

I would only have to pay back half of the money borrowed and I would have the following five years to do just that.

I knew that my dad didn't work anymore. He had developed emphysema and could no longer manage his carpentry work. They only had social security to live on. I could pay for my own wedding. I had saved. Maybe that's what gave me the power to decide the way it was going to be.

It would be very small. Not many relatives would travel to an out of town wedding, and most were still living in New Jersey. My aunt and uncle had moved up to our town after the death of my grandmother, eight years previously. I was sure that they would be there.

We, my fiancée and I, pulled into the driveway and parked the car beneath the cedar tree. I had so often swung on the board swing attached to the lower branch. The thick, twisted supporting ropes looked as durable as ever.

As we opened the car doors, Mom came out of the front door to give us both a hug. That was automatic for Mom. I thought that it was a fine way to greet people. I was comfortable hugging people, too. That's what I was used to seeing, though I never saw Mom and Dad give each other a hug. The greeting to other relatives was always there and special. It said, "Welcome to our home. I'm glad you're here."

After our greetings were exchanged, we proceeded inside through the screen door. I heard its abrupt closure, indicative of my mood. My dad was standing there.

"Hello," he said without a smile.

"Hello," I answered.

There was no gesture from him for a hug so I didn't offer

one. My fiancée, Tom, stepped toward him, smiling and putting his hand out for a shake. My dad reciprocated.

"Hello, Mr. Havas," Tom said, still all smiles.

"Hello," Dad responded, straight-faced but polite.

"Well, lunch is all ready," Mom said. "Why don't we eat and visit a little before you have to return? How is the job hunting going, Tom?"

And so the conversation went, first discussing job possibilities, then Tom's parents' health, then how my school year had ended, then graduate courses I would be taking during the summer.

My brother wasn't around and that disappointed me. I guess he felt that this should be a more private time, discussing an upcoming wedding and all.

With the meal finished, Tom got up from the table. "I'm going to take the car out for a drive; there were some strange sounds I heard on the way down. I want to be sure that it's all okay, and I know you all have things to discuss. I'll be back in a while. Thank you for the lunch, Mrs. Havas."

"You're welcome, Tom," Mom said. "You're not going to stay?"

"No. I really need to check out those sounds I heard. I'll be back." With that he was gone.

"So," I began, "we've set the date for the wedding—August 14th. That'll be two weeks before I have to go back to work. And the ceremony will be at St. Alphonsus Church in the town where I'm teaching."

"What!" Dad exclaimed.

"I've come to know the pastor there and I work with the

CYO," I explained in a tone that was not asking their permission. It was providing information. "Many of my students belong to the CYO and I plan to invite them to the ceremony if they'd like to come. I really want to get married *there*."

"I don't like it," Dad stated, with his face taking on a reddish hue.

Without comment, I continued. "Tom isn't Catholic. He's Episcopalian but Father said that was acceptable and we'd work around that in the ceremony. He would not have to convert," I said, realizing that my two sisters had not gone outside the faith in their choice of husbands. Another big difference—not the home parish *and* not of the same faith. Oh well. I was on a roll. Why stop now?

"And I want both you and Mom to walk me down the aisle," I added, holding my breath as my gaze shifted from my mom to my dad. Dad didn't look very well. He was resting his chin in his hands, elbows resting on the table.

His face was constricted and getting redder as each second ticked by. All of a sudden, he gripped the table with both hands. Then he began to slowly erupt like a volcano, building in strength and volume until he finally BLEW with a string of curses and swear words, spewing like molten lava from his mouth.

My heart took an immediate dive—now an all too familiar feeling. At the same time, the dam burst and tears started flowing.

I immediately stood up and walked out of the room, out of the house, speaking not a word.

I should have known. I should have been prepared. Why did I even consider the possibility that they would be excited about my marriage? Why? Why couldn't Dad just honor my desires for once? Why did he always have to be against what I wanted? I made my way across the lawn, tears cascading down my cheeks as my chest was racked with sobs.

Nothing was going to change the way I wanted it to be. NOTHING! Not this time.

I turned to see Mom making her way toward me. I stood there as she approached, a cold stillness overcoming the turmoil within me.

"Debby, Debby, shame on you for feeling that way." She was speaking with a tone in her voice that I had heard so many times growing up. Shame, shame, shame. Mom was big on shame.

"He means well," she said still with the tone. *How could she support what had just happened?*

"I hate him," I said as I tightened up inside, frozen at the mere thought of him.

"Don't say that," she replied, her tone riddled with *I am ashamed of you.*

She slowly turned away, shaking her head from side to side, and made her way back to the house. I looked after her as she moved across the lawn. I felt disappointed . . . so disappointed. *Where was the arm around my shoulder or a hug? Was I crazy for thinking that a mom, my mom, would have tried to console me in that way? Where had I gotten THAT idea?*

I turned down the path I had so often traveled as a child, seeking refuge in the woods, in Nature. I made my way to the stream that I frequented years ago. There I would sit upon a rock at the stream's edge where the water was deepest. Often, I would sing my songs with a loud, clear voice.

This time I made my way to a grassy spot on the edge of a bank. I was immediately aware of the gurgling sounds of the water moving over and around the rocks which were standing still and solid in its midst, undisturbed.

As I looked further downstream, my eyes began to focus on a small waterfall that had been formed by the leaves and mud trapped there, collecting layer upon layer, building a kind of dam for the water. Yet, the water had found its way over the block, forming a beautifully smooth little waterfall. I slowly lowered myself onto the moss cushion that had grown beside it.

Hadn't I experienced something similar?

I had collected many layers, not of leaves and mud but of another type of debris—disappointment, dislike and now hatred for my father, each layer building upon the previous until a wall had been constructed. I had built the wall so strong and tall that not even winds with the force of a hurricane could displace a mere fiber of it.

Could I, someday, conquer the height of that wall and become a beautiful waterfall flowing over it, journeying onward to the rest of my life, even appreciating the block that had formed, that I had built? Would I become stronger for it, for that experience? Would I become more accepting, more understanding and more compassionate?

Closing my eyes, I sat there, attempting to blend in with the sounds, becoming one with what was constant and consistent, not at all like my home life had been these past twenty-two years.

My father's disapproval spoke to me of there being only one way to have a relationship with the Divine. I had come to believe, along the way, that there were many and that had been the basis for creating my wedding ceremony the way that I had. Obviously, he hadn't accepted that. *Why am I not surprised?* I thought.

I wondered how it felt to be caressed by the water, caressed by anything or anyone. *Would I ever know that feeling? That touch so intimate that I would feel my very soul expand in ecstasy?*

Someday . . . maybe someday.

I sat there for a long, long time—until, in the far distance, I heard a car turning into our driveway. I aroused myself from my reverie, my respite. I gave thanks to that little collection of mud and leaves that had spoken so intimately to me. I had gained insight and hope. This was *my* journey. I could now proceed with hope for the future, *my* future, *my* wedding.

As I returned to the house, Tom was beginning to get out of the car. We would soon be leaving.

"How did it go?" he asked.

"I'll tell you about it on the ride home. Let's say our good-byes," I replied. "Is the car okay?"

"Yes, it's fine," he answered.

We entered the house as my mom came from the kitchen. "How's the car?" she asked.

"It's fine. We'll make it back with no problem," Tom answered confidently.

"I'm glad," she said, giving him her full attention.

I moved closer to her and extended my arms for a cursory hug. She reciprocated warmly as always.

"Good-bye, Mom," I said. "We'll talk soon."

"Yes," she said as if nothing had happened.

Dad was watching television in the living room. "Good-bye,

Dad," I called, my voice absent of emotion.

He did not get up but called from the other room, "Good-bye." *Was that embarrassment evident in his voice?* Tom said his good-byes and, after a hug from my mom, we left.

Driving out of the driveway, I realized another layer of my self-worth had been torn away that day. *How many layers are there left to go?* I wondered.

I had experienced neither respect nor acceptance, much less discussion of my wishes. I felt like a woman condemned. It seemed as though I would never experience that support, encouragement and love that I needed from my parents.

All of a sudden, the realization came thundering down to me yet again . . . *I am on my own.*

The memory of that day was so vivid. I remembered everything about it, every detail. I again picked up my pen and wrote from my heart, trying to return to an open, more positive state of presence.

Dad, you always put people down so you could appear better than they. Your identity was wrapped up in big cars and a daughter (my sister) *going to college–a façade, a face.*

I remember when you packed your suitcase and started walking down the road (after an argument with Mom). *I watched out the window and felt no sadness at all. I don't remember you coming back. But let's face it; without us you'd have no one to control and dominate and then where would your identity be?*

You didn't come back out of love. You came back out of survival.

I again put down my pen and looked out at the water. I felt the gentleness of the summer breeze and heard the sound of the wind through the white pines. I took a deep breath and exhaled slowly. I realized how tight and constricted my muscles had become during the reliving of my memories. I felt them begin to relax as I took another deep breath . . . and exhaled slowly . . . another deep breath . . . and exhaled slowly.

It was time to let go—let go of it all.

I felt drained, emptied of all emotion. A release had just occurred within me. I had said it all, telling Dad how I felt at each memory of hurt, putting it in the form of a letter to him in my journal. I knew, though, that I wasn't quite finished.

"I need to turn this around a bit, begin a positive outlook," I said aloud. "Help me now to understand the person you were, Dad, the reason for the changes. Help me to feel your hurts." With that said, I closed my eyes.

A scene flashed before me, a scene I *knew* I had not ever witnessed before. I saw my dad sitting in a straight back chair with a thick iron chain wrapped around him. His hands were crisscrossed, gripping opposite shoulders.

"Dad, are you in bondage?" I asked.

He didn't answer. I looked at his face, into his eyes. There I saw sadness, regret and shame. Was it his awareness of his actions over the years that had caused his bondage? Or was it *my* hatred of him that had so bound his spirit? *Was it* my *lack of forgiveness?* I wondered.

"Do you love me, Dad?" I asked.

The lingering question that every child needs to know the

answer to—was she loved? That was *all* that was wanted. That was *all* that was needed. I needed that answer, too.

Again, he didn't answer. I felt sadness, regret and shame.

I noticed dragonflies skimming over the water, darting here and there, going about their purpose. Was I going about my purpose, too? Only time would tell. I became aware that all my energy seemed to have left me. *Maybe this is enough for today,* I thought and rose to leave.

Gathering my backpack and water, I dragged myself down the path, feeling depleted and down, my father's chained image implanted on my brain. *I know there is a lot more to deal with,* I thought as I continued down the trail. *I wonder what tomorrow will bring.*

Tomorrow became today and I made my way to the board-walk earlier than usual. I loved the lake in the morning with the fog lifting. It spoke to me of peace, quiet, calmness—Nature's testimony that all was well.

Though I usually sat and looked out at the lake, today I stood and became part of the scene before me, feeling as if I was being lifted, too: one with the fog ... drifting ... floating. What a wonderful feeling. I remained watching until the fog left and the mountains became visible again. The blue sky greeted me with the warm light of sunshine.

I turned slowly and stared at the falls which the outlet formed. There I saw a fish jumping upward.

Over and over again it attempted to reach the lake waters. It kept on trying until it made it.

Was the same thing happening to me as I tried to forgive my dad for the past? I felt the healing was coming in little steps of forgiveness. I knew that if I could understand more of what his life had been like for him, it would help with my being able to forgive.

As I turned around, I saw the fish swimming in the lake water.

"Are you the same one that kept trying to jump the falls a few minutes ago?" I asked. "You must be tired. That took a lot of energy to keep trying, knowing the lake is where you wanted to go, *needed* to go."

Standing there, watching the fish, I realized this was where *I* needed to go. I had been stuck in my childhood perceptions *all these years.*

As I sat, I dug out my pen and journal from my backpack and began to write what came to me from my heart. I was again writing to my dad, continuing the letter I had begun yesterday.

June 27

Dear Dad,

You were an unhappy person whose pride would not allow others to help. You would never ask; they could not offer. You began to fail at being the bread-winner of the family. Pride did not allow you to let Mom work anymore at Christmastime. You couldn't stand the fact that Mom had her own money, even though she only spent it on the family.

All of a sudden, it was like I was inside my dad's head and heart, thinking his thoughts, feeling his hurts. The saga continued.

You were embittered by having to contribute to the support of your brothers so they could go to college and get jobs—an opportunity you never had. You ended up with little money and little employment.

You could not speak loving words or show any gestures of love unless bringing home a pay check was your way of showing love. I needed more than that from you.

It must have hurt your pride when Buddy bought things for Mom that you couldn't afford. He became your rival. Your control over him was gone. He bought Mom the washer, the dryer, the television, poured the cement floor in the basement for her and even had a fur stole made for her from the nutrias he had raised and skinned himself.

I know the worst thing that can happen to me is for someone to lose respect for me. You had that happen with two people, two adults who were close to you—your wife and your son.

I feel badly that you never got to know me, nor I, you. I could have cheered you with my smiles, my excitement and love for life, the discoveries I made and, of course, my hugs. There's nothing like a child's hugs to make it all worth it.

I would like to hug you now, Daddy, and hold you and tell you that I love you. I understand so much more.

I would like to tell you I forgive you for not being the affirming, loving parent I needed then. I forgive you for not showing your love affectionately to me or praising my successes. Will you forgive me for becoming so insensitive to your needs and for not trying to give or risk giving you a hug?

I remember I was in college, my junior year. We were riding in the front seat of the car. You and Mom had come down for a visit. I was sitting next to the window with Mom in the center. You tossed a bag onto my lap. You didn't hand it to me or say anything, just tossed it. The one present you ever bought me. Mom told me later that you picked the earrings out yourself—my birthstone. Maybe that does say a lot, remembering the day I was born. I never thought of it that way before but that was your way of trying, wasn't it?

I remember my comment, "What's the occasion?" That sounds so sarcastic now. What I was really saying was, "It's too late. Why not all those birthdays?"

You never told me how sick you really were then. I think you realized that I did matter to you and you wanted to begin again. It was I who said, "No!"

I would never want to be judged as I judged

you. I kept them (the earrings) for a while and then I almost put them in a garage sale to spite you. They were so meaningless to me. But I think I kept them— the only gift you ever gave me, but it said a whole lot. I was just unable to read the message. If I'd only had as forgiving a heart as my daughter. I hope I still have them. Please let them be at my house.

I'm sorry Daddy. I'm really sorry. I want to wear them. I really do.

Can you forgive me? Please, somehow, show me that you can forgive me, too.

My gaze drifted outward over the water, as I watched the wakes a passing canoe had created. They approached the place where I was sitting, becoming smaller and smaller until they didn't even exist. Is that what was happening to the pent-up hurts and resentments I had been carrying?

If I could rid myself of them, could I lift the bonds of hatred for my father from my very soul? I knew I needed to understand more of what Dad's inner life had been like—those dreams that had never been realized, those disillusions and failed attempts.

You felt unappreciated and unloved, didn't you, Dad, when you were young? And taken for granted? Used? Remember you gave life to the four of us, (your children). Each of us has helped other people. We've had our own children. One of us has risked his life fighting for freedom, the same freedom that led your parents and Mom's parents to bring you both to this country years ago.

Your blood flows through us and through our children. I'm proud of that. My own stubbornness has grown into determination and strength, even the strength of being so easily able to share my feelings.

Thank you, Dad, for all you did give me; that which flows through me and that which I am to become. I love you. Peace.

The wind had picked up, blowing my long brown hair across my face. I attempted to sweep it back into place and lost some of it again. I knew I had to catch it, put it all back in place. Suddenly, I was struck by a thought.

I wanted to pay my own way for college. I wanted to pay for my own wedding. Is that the same way Dad wanted to support his family himself? Was it due to his pride that he couldn't ask for help or his need for control?

I recall how hard it was for me, when my hand didn't work anymore, to ask for help. It was humbling but it helped me to realize how important having control had become to me. It must not have been easy for you, either, Dad, needing help to breathe (in your later years, due to your emphysema) and then allowing people to help you. I understand that, Dad. I have that problem, too, admitting that I am wrong or that I can't do something.

Admitting I was wrong seemed to broadcast the notion of weakness where being right radiated strength. My husband tended to laugh when I made a mistake and then it seemed more like a failure, like *I* was a failure. But it was the *mistake* he was laughing at and not me, personally, in most cases. I did need help in remembering that. *I have the* right *to make mistakes. It is my privilege and I accept it.*

The wind was blowing harder. Actually it had grown to the strength of a gale. *Time to pick up and go back.* As I moved quickly down the forest path, I felt the first droplets of rain on my face. I became aware of the tinkling sound as rain struck the quaking aspen leaves above my head. *I feel so tired. I think I'll take a nap after lunch today.*

I awoke from my nap with a clear thought. At mass, the priest had said *that we tend to cling to things and other people for our identity and we need to learn to detach. He said that adolescence is a stage of lowest self-image which is why peer pressure becomes so important to them. They are their friends, their possessions, their clothes. He said that many people never learn to detach.*

Wow! I realized that *I* had never learned to detach. Was it because I wasn't allowed to experience that stage? I missed out on having friends over, staying overnight at someone's house and being part of a group of friends in junior high or high school. I'd always wanted a best friend. I realized that I felt a jealousy when someone I called a friend had other friends, too. I was an adult, yet I was still attaching. What an awareness!

I didn't need fancy clothes and preferred a more simple life, as far as possessions go. I would have to say that, until more recently, friends had seemed more important to me than aunts, uncles and cousins did. At least I'd *begun* to detach. *Friendships are important but no longer vital to me. They help to make me feel complete but I won't die without any one of them. Many people moved on, after their teen years, from their peer groups back to family. I was beginning to move on, too, and it was beginning with Dad.*

After supper I was drawn to the dock in front of the retreat house. The wind had subsided, all had calmed and quieted. I thought of silence and how loudly silence could speak—between people—between Dad and myself. Silent relationships could be quite positive as two people could almost know each other's thoughts and be very comfortable with each other. Speaking for Dad's and my relationship, however, his act of ignoring me told me that I wasn't *worthy* of acknowledgment. My not speaking to *him* said that he didn't *deserve* to know what was going on in my life.

With pen in hand, I began to write . . .

Silence . . .silence . . . .
So much to say,
So much to hear,
Silence . . . .
Did you catch it?
Did I speak?
Silence . . . .
Do you understand?
How do I say it?
Silence . . . .
Surely you must know,
Of course you do.

Silence . . . .
Silence is that which goes unspoken,
Words of the heart so often hidden.
Yet—
    Caring . . .
      Sharing . . .
        Deep
          Deep
            Down.
Fear!
  Risk!
    Acceptance?
      Rejection?
Neither you nor I shall wear the crown.

I had said it all—the price Dad and I had paid for silence. We couldn't get those years back. They were lost to us. But we could begin right *then* to have a special relationship. *Since you have passed on, it will be a challenge for us both.* I thought. *But I believe* anything *is possible.*

It had been raining hard all morning. Although I loved to walk in the rain, this had been a downpour and so I stayed inside and watched the clouds moving across the sky, thundering their way overhead as they passed. Their shapes changed, coloring changed, even the rate of movement changed.

Was I changing, too? *I certainly need to.* I felt listless, groggy, as if I were drifting—but to where?

Always there are questions. *Maybe a nap will help revive me,*

I thought as I proceeded upstairs to my room.

I awoke from my nap, startled. Grabbing my pen and journal I wrote the words as they came pouring out onto the page.

June 28

A parcel tossed upon my lap,
I gave it not much thought,
The bag—brown paper,
A word not said,
What emotions had it wrought?

Surprise? Confusion? Resentment?
At a gift so harshly given.
Yet, tucked inside,
Two yellow jewels,
A prize worthy of heaven.

Do I have them? Did I wear them?
What was my answer then?
If I only knew,
If I only knew,
The message hidden within.

If I knew then what I know now,
How rich I'd have been, indeed.
The joy I'd have felt,
The gladness I'd have known
Having a Dad who could say, "I'm sorry."

"I'm sorry for all those times in the past
That I'd hurt you so, my child
By not hugging,

By not holding,
By not helping you to smile.

No, I was harsh and strict and cold,
Not the tender love you needed.
The tears I held
So deep inside
For the hugs I sorely needed.

Life was unfair to each of us—
No work, my illness, my pride.
Your needs so deep,
The risk so great,
My love I chose to hide.

I withheld that tender love
And you withheld your smile.
And so each day,
We grew apart,
Who could tell we were Father and child?

You always had a stubborn streak,
Now it's called determination.
Believe it or not,
You got that from me.
Is not that cause for celebration?

And your love for music, I had that, too,
Although you never saw it.
I forgot how to sing,
I forgot how to dance,
Life's music got dismal without it.

Your dark-colored skin and dark brown eyes—
A cutie beyond measure.
I never knew,

How deep within,
The jewels that were in my treasure.

The day I gave the gift to you,
But you didn't read the message.
It was too late,
I knew it then,
Even I couldn't miss that message.

So strong had I built that wall between us
Every day, every step of the way.
How often I'd wished
It would topple right down,
But I'd built it on rock not clay.

The rock of anger and jealousy,
Of domination and pride and control.
I wanted to be
So important to you,
I guess I misread my role.

For what you needed, as I know now,
Was someone to hold you and say,
"I love you, Debby,
My little one."
That's all I had to say.

I love you, dear, you were my own,
There, I've finally said it.
Draw close to me now,
I'm with you here,
Never, ever, forget it."

I reread the poem that had burst forth from the depths, the depths of *me*, from my very soul. As I did, the tears also burst forth like the downpour of the morning's rain. I felt like I was crying out all the disappointments, all the hurt, all the pain of my childhood and beyond. I took ownership of *my* part in prolonging the negative feelings by *not* forgiving, *not* understanding, before now, what my father had been going through.

As I shared the poem with my spiritual director, the flood of tears began again. The flow was steady, becoming more forceful as I heard my father's voice coming through the words. My spiritual director felt that it wasn't a coincidence that the person speaking had changed from me to Dad.

"I feel like it's Dad speaking to me," I said.

"I agree with you," he replied.

After I left his room at the close of my session, I found a quiet place to sit and reflect on his words to me. Before me was a large window where I saw nothing but sky. My thoughts came tumbling out in poetry form. Quickly, I took out my pen to record the words.

Silence is a bondage all its own,
Now we've said what we had to say.

You've spoken to me and I've spoken to you
Words not said along the way.

The time that's passed we can't relive,
Life's kind of strange that way.

We just go forward, knowing we forgive,
Happy we had our say.

I know I'm a better person now
Than I was yesterday.

I thank you, Father, I thank you, Dad
For lighting my pathway.

The rain had stopped as I again wandered out to the falls. It was cooler and the air smelled fresh and clean. I, too, felt cleansed and refreshed. I had told my spiritual director about the image of Dad in chains and how it had made me feel. He suggested I visualize the scene again. I knew just where I needed to be.

The boardwalk had dried quickly from the wind blowing across it, so I sat down with pen and paper ready. I closed my eyes and conjured up the image of Dad in chains and I held it there. I began to feel his pain . . . or was it *my* pain?

As I stayed with Dad's pain, I realized that there was *another figure near him also in chains. My focus changes as I try to see who it is. It's me! I am chained the same way. I begin to notice a figure (Jesus) drawing near to us. First He moves to Dad and begins to unwrap him, encircling him, around and around. I see Dad's face begin to relax and a slight smile forms. He begins to radiate warmth. I can feel it.*

When Dad is freed, the figure moves to me and unwraps me in the same pattern. As Dad and I stand, we look at each other, warmth and love flowing through our eyes. I bask in a lifetime of love. He opens his arms as I move to him and we embrace. Taking hold of each other's hand, we begin to walk.

We are at a field of flowers, where trees and green grass line the edge. Dad sits down on a rock. I am a child now, holding a basket I am filling with the wild flowers I'm picking—daisies and buttercups. I arrange them in my basket and bring them to show him. I am skipping and bouncing as I go. He smiles and holds that look in his eyes, relaxed and happy, spending time with me.

I see dragonflies and run off to chase them, laughing and frolicking. I return with one of them on my finger and I show it to him. That lingering smile and love in his eyes are precious. His expression doesn't change, for he's soaking it in, too.

Now Jesus is there. Dad and He begin to fade back. The same look remains as Dad and I stare at each other. I am there, alone now, with my basket of flowers and realize that the dragonfly has come to rest on my left shoulder. I am not sad. I am not regretful. I am at peace.

I do not know if all of Dad's chains are broken but I do know that he is freer than before and I, too, am freer than before. How wonderful that the dragonfly I shared my walk with days ago returned in the scene with my Dad.

Closure indeed.

Forgiveness is a process. It does not always happen with the flip of a switch. Years of ignoring a child is not necessarily healed overnight. Nor are the years of hatred destroyed in a moment, but the process had begun. Great strides had been made by both Dad and me.

Dad's spirit had spoken. That was the bondage. He needed to tell me and show me how much he cared by allowing me to recall the memory of the earrings, by letting me see what was in his heart. I knew that he was freer and it was up to me to forgive him.

The child within me says, "I'll never forget." The adult says, "I want to forgive." Both are possible. They are not a contradiction.

Forgiving is not an act of weakness but of strength. It is a choice that I had consciously made. I accepted that this hurt had happened, but I would not allow myself to feel victimized. I chose to not be harmed any longer by the hatred I had carried. I would not allow it. It had affected my peace, my happiness and my wholeness. It had placed a block in my relationships with family, friends and co-workers.

It had skewed my expectations of others and myself. *If I had been hurt by someone,* I wondered, *was she even aware that she had hurt me? Was it even her intention to do that? She might not have been experiencing anything at all. She may not even have known what her action had destroyed in me.* I was *choosing* to feel this way and I was the one being slowly destroyed by it. Therefore, I *chose* to let in the Light, only the Light.

I chose to forgive.

Weeks had passed since retreat ended. I found that when I thought of Dad, I experienced a warm feeling beginning to grow inside me, and a slight smile dressed my lips. I was beginning to *like* my dad, yes, even *love* my dad. And I was beginning to notice that when I thought of God as Father, I no longer felt distance and judgment but rather tenderness and kindness—all great gifts of that retreat.

All made possible through the act of forgiveness.

13

BETRAYED

all was quickly approaching. I was at home, having been rejected for a full-time teaching position. I had worked at the parochial school for fourteen years previously, in a part-time position. With me, however, nothing was part-time. I had given my responsibilities full-time effort and energy. I had been able to share some of my disappointment at my silent retreat, but I later realized that the real issue for me was a feeling of betrayal. There it was again. I felt that I had given my all to the school and to the children, in a part-time capacity.

But I wasn't 'good enough' to be hired full-time.

The school's decision made me feel as if I had been branded with no backup support. My husband chose silence on the issue. Even though the programs I had run were evaluated as excellent by the administration, there was genuine concern by the interview committee that I would not be able to finish out the year. It made me feel as if I were being judged; that the position of full-time teacher would be *too much* for me, based on my glaring diagnosis of five years before.

Both my primary care physician and my neurologist had told me that my improvement had grown to a point where they felt I was ready to consider full-time teaching. Yet, with Multiple Sclerosis, no matter how much better I became, that label followed me and gave an unrealistic impression of my capability.

I knew that same impression would follow me wherever I went. That is, if people knew. So, in the future I would need to be very selective with whom I told.

Being disappointed at not being hired full-time is one issue, but I felt *betrayed* and that emotion holds a much stronger reaction, I knew. *But why did I feel betrayed? Where had that come from?*

I felt my body had betrayed me when I was diagnosed, but there was yet another memory begging to come forward. I was taken back in time.

One summer, about ten years earlier, my husband and I found ourselves stepping into the role of co-directors of a summer youth camp. He was then a deacon and this was our call to a special ministry.

I had originally experienced a strong inner prompting for my husband's entering the Deaconate program and so I gave my support, thinking this would somehow aid our stressful marriage. After all, it was a religious venture, and I knew there were gifts to be shared, albeit *hidden* deep within him.

I now felt that same strong inner prompting to accept this position at camp. At least that's what my intuition was leading me to do. But should I?

What am I going to learn from this? I wondered. One moment, I felt excited about this venture and the next moment I felt anxious, fearful of failure, fearful that I wouldn't know what to do and fearful of the unknown. If I thought about it long enough, I began to be overwhelmed by all these fears.

It was as if I was absolutely sure I would fail. For just a brief moment, I wondered where that idea came from. I'd had successes in my life, so where was this deeper "certainty" of failure coming from?

As the wife of a Catholic Deacon, I was given the opportunity to have a spiritual director. That allowed me to have a monthly visit from Sister Catherine, who had a background in counseling. She scheduled me into her visits to convents in the diocese. She had instructed all the deaconate wives to take the Myers-Briggs Personality Inventory.

It was this woman who helped me begin my journey into the unknown; that is the unknown territory inside Deborah Diane—me. It was this woman who made it a point to tell me, "You have a wonderful intuitive gift. It is your strength. Believe in it. You will always be able to sense things that others cannot."

That was interesting. I'd always doubted myself when I felt or sensed what others were feeling.

I could walk into a room and know there was deep sadness present even though everyone was laughing. I could tell when people were hurting inside or angry or fearful, no matter what mask they tried to use to hide these emotions.

I had felt physical pain in my right shoulder when my mom was having an attack of her bursitis, even though she lived many towns away. I had a deep sense of loss at the *same* moment a friend's abusive dad passed from this earth, even though I hadn't known he was dying.

These were all things that I could share with Catherine and she never laughed at me or tried to make me feel that I was strange or *different*. She helped me to understand the gift and to accept what it was, which inspired me to follow the intuitive sense of calling. She also encouraged me to remember, in making a decision: *Always follow your heart and you can never go wrong*.

I took away these valuable words and began to incorporate them into my daily life.

Still the deep self-doubt continued. I accepted the position at youth camp, because I felt I was being led to do so. Yet inwardly I wondered, *Can I handle it?* Why was some other voice whispering I would fail?

As a family, we lived at the camp full-time. The girls were four and six then. We were responsible for twelve staff, campers, and all programs that were offered. It was a fantastic summer, in my estimation. Most of the staff were brand new and were either of college age or had joined the work force, one even planning to go into the Armed Forces. For the summer, the girls inherited twelve brothers and sisters, and they blossomed from all the attention and varied talents shared with them, as did I.

Very quickly, I felt accepted, respected, even admired. Father Carl was overseeing our work and he was often present at the camp. I found him to be very competent and personal, making good use of his gifts. I was delighted when he recognized and made me aware of the gifts *I* was bringing to this camp community. He encouraged me to use them, giving me the utmost support.

It was wonderful—the feeling that the presence of freedom allowed. In our frequent discussions, he noted my open-mindedness. In my whole life, no one had recognized that gift or told me of it. He spoke to me about what a responsible person I was, noted my organizational skills and my creativity. He made mention of my spirituality which was expressed through my liturgical dance, the daily use of my intuitive gift as I dealt with the interpersonal issues of the staff, my sense of humor and the fact that I was a great mom to my girls.

I thrived.

I enjoyed supervising the programs and building community among the staff. On weekends, when the cook was off, I became the food creator and organizer, making homemade granola and bagels for all of them. It was fun! On Sundays, we all went to church together. We swam together, had cookouts and shared about our personal lives—thoughts, perceptions and philosophies. And a staff community became a reality.

I discovered that I could direct, in a nonthreatening way, changes I wished to make, and my requests were respected and followed. Staff seemed comfortable sharing personal struggles with me.

I realized I was good at listening, and guiding them in considering possible solutions, if I so deemed. Sometimes, listening was enough as they talked out their concerns. They often came to their own solutions or realized that there wasn't any solution at all. Maybe they couldn't change the situation and just needed to accept it as it was. It was a role I found very gratifying.

The summer progressed with its own challenges among the campers and within the staff, but we worked it all out together and the summer program was a success. I didn't see much of my husband, though he functioned where he was needed and I did the same. The summer did not bring us closer as a couple, as I had hoped, but we had shared a unity of purpose—a successful camp experience for all. And it had been, hadn't it?

At the end of the summer, each of the staff had an evaluation session with Father Carl. I was a little anxious going in, but he agreed with me that the summer had been a success. Great! We *had* done it! I felt delighted and relieved, having always wondered what he really thought. I was ready to hear that he was recommending our returning for the following summer.

He followed his report of the successes with his final comment, "I am not going to recommend your return for another summer as co-directors. After much consideration, I feel the experience has been too stressful on your marriage."

My heart immediately sank. It felt like it had been torn in two, my insides ripped apart. If he said anything more, I didn't hear it, *couldn't* hear it. I imploded. I went totally within myself, into the lonely realms of Deborah Diane once again. I saw nothing there as I wandered from room to room in my heart . . . in my soul. I felt embarrassed and ashamed at my failure, and I took it personally, so very personally.

How could I have been so wrong in thinking all my hard work and sacrifice would earn me the reward of being told they wanted me back? How could I have been so wrong in thinking I had actually made forward strides in the area of self-confidence? Were the results of using my gifts *really* positive as I thought I'd witnessed? Had it actually all been a failure? I clung to the hope that it hadn't *all* been a failure, that *I* hadn't been a total failure. Yet, for me, a person with a poor self-image, it was a horrific blow.

I was no longer needed, no longer necessary. It was like all I had gained had been tossed out the window and I hadn't *had* that choice, hadn't *made* that choice. Someone else had.

My husband didn't seem as tormented as I by the decision. He was not into sharing feelings much and had little patience for mine. So, I was on my own, carrying my own burden with all of my questions rolling around inside my head. Then there were all of the voices inside my head adding to the chorus, telling me what a fool I'd been to even *think* that I had some worth and gifts to share with others. And the pride I'd felt as I saw my endeavors come to fulfillment; that was wrong. Pride was wrong. It was like all these voices were competing for the podium but the audience was limited to one—*me*.

In actuality, only one voice won out, despite all of my effort and hard work. It wasn't good *enough* and *I wasn't good enough.*

I carried that ache within me all the time, and felt it pulling me down, deeper and deeper. It was a constant struggle to keep above it. When I met other people, I felt a withdrawal inward, a sinking sensation. I felt entirely alone in my suffering. There was no one with whom I could share it. Only being with my girls could lift me up. Only the hours I was with them was I *free* of it all.

Suddenly, I saw a connection between the betrayals I had felt at summer camp and the saga of the transparent, yellow plastic pig of long ago when I was a girl. The money in the piggy bank had been stolen by someone in authority, my father. I had had no choice in the matter. It said to me that anyone could break in and take something from me at any time, and they had. It had happened again!

I had invested my*self* in that summer camp experience—my time, my talents, my abilities, my *presence*—and nickel by nickel, I had filled the bank to the top. As the bank had filled, so had I; my self-confidence, my self-image and my self-esteem had all taken an upward shot. The opportunity to have the *freedom* to develop these qualities in a loving, supportive atmosphere was now gone.

So, the qualities I had built up tumbled, too. But I had *allowed* myself to feel that way, to react in the same extremely intense way, this time in response to not being rehired. It had been an automatic reaction for me. The spark had been ignited again.

Now that I recognized it, I could begin to affect a change in future reactions to similar situations. I could *choose* not to react that way. It would take practice, but it *was* possible.

That was how I felt at *that* time and, yet, here I was again, experiencing that heart-wrenching tearing in my soul at not being hired for a full-time position at school.

The more I thought about it, I had become aware over the years that our not continuing to be co-directors was in the best interest of everyone. Our marriage was not a solid, loving relationship. We were two good people with gifts to share, but summer camp would no longer be the place to share them.

No one knew what was going on inside of me. No one *could* have known or understood the infection that had been festering all of my life, the infection that had taken root before I was born. Many events had promoted a slow growth of that infection and, at the time, no antibiotic yet discovered could conquer it.

We had been at camp for one summer only and shared our gifts to the fullest. I grew tremendously that summer, as did many. For that I was grateful and forever thankful. Though it ended painfully at the time, I *had* come full circle to a feeling of warmth and understanding at the memory of summer camp.

Life and events moved on. The scar tissue on my soul was forgotten, but it was not without its own power. It became a burden that I would carry for a long, long time.

My experience at camp had triggered, yet again, my experience of long ago: working hard, achieving a goal, and being devastated by someone's reaction, someone significant. In high school it had been my mother. In my camp experience, it had been someone I had dared to call *friend.* In my adult life, there were very few, indeed, who gained that status from *my* viewpoint. I had learned to be private at a young age and trust was hard to come by.

Though my façade had slowly grown over the years, my needs had only deepened, changing little. I had many acquaintances in my life, but could I continue with only those?

I yearned for a *true* friend, *one . . . true . . . friend.*

The school's decision not to hire me full-time had reopened a can of worms. All of these episodes where I had felt betrayed had been laid at my feet. It was my choice. Did I crush them once and for all or step over them and leave them lying there to infiltrate my heart and soul again? I decided to take action.

I had formally resigned a year before the full-time openings had appeared. People assumed it was because my health was so poor but that was incorrect. It had been a private issue that had precipitated the decision, as I had stated in my letter of resignation. Only one person knew the real reason—my husband. Again, he chose silence. Then I knew. He never would, never *could* speak up in my defense.

I was, at that time, beginning to climb the Adirondack High Peaks which are over 4000 feet in elevation. Physically, I felt good. I no longer experienced any numbness or loss of function. My previous strength and energy had returned. My faith continued to deepen. Somehow I knew there was a reason for all of this happening to me. But what was it? Would I ever know?

Still, I felt something *needed* to be said. *I* needed to say something to the school's Board of Education. So I drafted a letter to them, to recommend and educate them on the issue of their rejection of me.

I began by stating the reason for my correspondence and my background of qualifications. I also mentioned the positions of service I had held at the school. Then I stated the crux of my letter's purpose:

I could not honestly think of a reason for your not hiring me, knowing the person that I am and the job I have done. I was shocked at being informed that there was genuine concern for my health and my being able to finish out the year. I need to state that if this concern did exist, my doctor should have been formally contacted and the matter discussed with him. No one on the board is capable of judging the status of my health, presuming I would even apply if I felt that either my health would be endangered or that I could not be effective in the classroom and give 100% of myself to the children.

The board's not caring enough to find out the facts is the cause of my feelings of betrayal. I realize now that I will not be hired by you for a full-time position at any time.

Multiple Sclerosis does not mean incapable. I cannot change your impressions or misinformation about this disease. I simply ask, for the benefit of future applicants, that you never judge without information from the experts—the applicant and the doctor.

People's judgment of me based on the disease I live with is truly a heavier cross than the disease itself. The difference between me and another is that I do not push myself past what I feel is healthy for me. I have developed effective coping skills.

Another person does not know when or if he/she is going to have a heart attack or develop cancer. Do you not hire a person with diabetes or arthritis? Do you eliminate the truly positive effect these people may have on the children, not only because of the gifts they share but because they DO live with a chronic disease? What better witness is there to faith?

Do not eliminate people because you do not understand their physical conditions. Find out about them and do not go on presumptions. My personal interview did not indicate that MS was of major concern.

I truly believe that good can come out of any situation. I know that God is still with me and He will provide me with children to teach. I have no doubt.

Good luck in the future and consider your decisions carefully. The new people will do fine and we will all grow on this our journey. Please pray for me, as I will for you.

Immediately, I felt better. I welcomed peace back into my soul.

After rereading the letter, I typed it, postmarked it and sent it on its way with no expectations. I had achieved closure. I knew I had done all I could do in my own defense. There wasn't anyone else stepping forward to help.

Betrayal is an interesting emotion. It is what it is. There's no going back, at least not for me.

Receipt of the letter was never acknowledged. And it didn't really bother me. I had closure. I had peace. My time there was over. It was time to move on. The desire to teach at *that* school had disappeared entirely and I knew it would never return.

I was grateful for the experience of working with the children, learning from them while they learned from me. It was a fine experience to have taught my own daughters, too, first as their physical education teacher and secondly as their science and health teacher. I'll never regret those years at the parochial school.

So, I proceeded forward to whatever my future held at the time. I was *on my own* again, as I had been so many times in my life.

It actually became even clearer to me that I had *always* been on my own, *and that was okay.*

It was the here and now I had to deal with, and deal with that I *would.*

14

TURNING POINT

Throughout my adolescence, young adulthood and into my adulthood, a nightmare began to reoccur which I could not explain.

It was always nighttime in this dream and I was sleeping in my bed in the house where I grew up. My door was open, the light in the hallway shining dimly, casting shadows on the wall. All was still. All was silent.

I awoke and got out of bed, making my way very slowly to the doorway. I gazed toward my parents' bedroom, their door also being open.

There, I saw a man beside the bed by my mother. He was going through her pocketbook which rested on a small wooden table beside the head of the bed. I knew that he was after money to steal.

I wanted to cry out. I *needed* to cry out—to warn her and everyone in the house, but the words wouldn't come. I didn't have a voice. Not even '*Help!*' could escape from my lips. I tried again and again, each time more desperate than the last. The only sound that did escape was a low, mournful moan that went on and on like a funeral dirge. The sound of it would awaken me, quivering and quaking in my bed under my pink cotton bedspread.

This dream scared me to death. *Where is this dream coming from? What does it mean?*

"Please make it go away," I pleaded agonizingly to the air around me. But it would linger until exhaustion won out and I sank back into sleep.

During my college years, my roommates would awaken me at the horrific sound that would erupt at this part of my nightmare. I would apologize to them and everyone would fall back to sleep, eventually.

Finally, when I was in my forties, I attended a workshop on dreams where we were led to focus on a recent or recurring dream and further still, to focus on the most important item or person in the dream. I, of course, focused on my mother's purse and what was being stolen from it.

All of a sudden, the image of a transparent, yellow plastic pig standing high up on my father's dresser entered my mind and I knew. *I knew!* I dissolved in tears. Long, long minutes passed, as I relived the deep pain of loss.

Again I felt that life force of excitement that had been stolen from me by my dad that day. What an opportunity for both child and father to form a lasting bond and positive memory together. Instead, I had carried the pain all those years. It was deep. It was agonizing. I let it go, let it all go, feeling it very deeply as the final plunge of my soul was taken one last time. Down . . . down . . . down. It *was* the last time. I never again had that nightmare.

Many years later, as I reflected on that nightmare, I realized that the man by my mother's side of the bed, stealing from her purse, represented my dad. He had stolen everything from my mother that was of value to her. His behaviors had deprived her of her independence and his actions had eroded her self-confidence. He was, actually, a man insecure within himself. He was and *needed* to be the master of power and control.

During World War II, when rationing was a way of life, Mom had earned some income with a neighbor woman, embroidering flowers on sweaters. She did this without my father's permission or knowledge, imagining what his reaction would be. She truly loved doing it and was very skilled at the lovely needlework she created with fine, perfectly designed stitches.

The pennies she earned made it possible for my older brother and sister to attend the movies each Saturday morning, a real treat for any child at that time. They would receive a small bag of candy or a comic book, supplied by the theatre, as they left. What fun, at a not-so-much fun time!

"No more!" my father yelled at Mom when he found out. "Do you understand?" He forbade her to continue. The movie visits ceased as did her fine, perfectly designed stitches of embroidery on the sweaters.

After they moved to Watson, located at the outskirts of Lowville, a small department store in town needed extra help over the Christmas holidays. A neighbor who worked at the store suggested Mom help out.

"Rose," Stella began," Mr. Mack needs help in the store over the holidays and he told me he'd be delighted to have you try it. You can ride with me. We come right by the house. Why don't you try it?"

"Oh, I don't know, Stella. You know Steve," Mom replied.

"So?" she responded. "Tell him it will give you some money for Christmas. How can he refuse?" And so she began, until Dad, upon his return home at the end of the week, found out.

As usual, he began yelling at her, demanding she turn her check over to him. That was the only time I ever heard her refuse, reasoning with him that the moneys were going toward presents and extra food needed over the holidays.

Mom was a gentle soul. The owner of the store was impressed with how she interacted with customers and handled sales. Besides, she enjoyed working there. He wished to hire her for longer, but the time for *helping out* was over.

"No!" Dad yelled at her. "I said you are not returning!" He forbade her to continue. Her experience of feeling appreciated and valued at the store was over.

My dad seemed threatened by Mom's enjoying activities outside of the home. She *did* enjoy the activity, the social contact, and the income that she had opportunity to earn. She seemed happy. It was a taste of independence for her.

These experiences would help to build her self-confidence. All told, that threatened him. It threatened his power and control and *that* he could not handle. Her social contacts weaned. Neighbors moved away.

"Don't turn out dumb like me," Mom would tell me over and over again. She didn't think that she had any intelligence even though she had graduated from high school and Dad had only gone through the eighth grade.

I watched her lose any semblance of her personhood. She ceased attending Home Bureau, comprised of a group of women who gathered to sew, knit and crochet. She withdrew from the

Daughters of Isabella, a women's church organization. Again, Dad noticed her obvious pleasure with herself and the enjoyment she got being away from home. That grated on him. There were yearly dues to be paid and she didn't have any income other than his. The control was his and his alone.

In the beginning, she could save some money from my brother's rent which he paid her weekly. He boarded at home after the Korean War, having enlisted in the Air Force at age seventeen, with Mom's signature to escape those frequent beatings from Dad.

Over the years, Dad's treatment of Mom and his demands ate away at her ability to be affectionate toward her children, and even her ability to *receive* affection from anyone. She felt she just didn't deserve it.

I thought more about her response to receiving a gift. "Oh, you shouldn't have done that," was the common one. The action seemed to embarrass her. Instead of experiencing gladness and joy at the surprise and thoughtfulness, I witnessed shame as she accepted it, her serious gaze moving downward, instead of a delighted smile reaching toward the heavens.

For, in her eyes, she didn't *need* anything. She didn't *want* anything. She didn't *deserve* anything. Her needs and wants had been denied. Her desires had ceased to exist. Her dreams had been lost along the way.

What were my *dreams?* I asked myself. I was NOT going to let *them* get lost.

Before I knew it, another June had arrived with azure blue skies filled with cotton ball clouds that piled one on top of another. The darting sun popped out now and again as if to remind me not to give up, *never* give up on life. There were days when darkened clouds seemed to dominate my life and times when brilliant sun was all I saw. I chose to focus on the sunny times, and that became my philosophy. It enabled me to endure those cloudy days when it seemed my world had taken an abrupt change in course.

So, here I was again on my eight-day silent retreat. This time I wasn't on the shore of Lake Placid but in a residential area of Syracuse, New York. As I neared Christ the King Retreat House, I consciously began to rid myself of any expectations of what I might be led to deal with *this* time. Still, I wondered, *would it be some issue I was trying to deal with in my present or would it be something from my past, my ancient past?*

And what's more, *would I have the strength to endure the pain of facing it again?* I wasn't sure.

I awaited the surprises this retreat had in store for me with anticipation. I knew there would be some tough times as I tried to confront the hidden truths as I became aware of them, but I also knew that I would learn and grow in awareness and understanding of myself. I needed to remain open to any and all challenges. Needless to say, there were many areas in my life I *could* concentrate on. Better to leave it to the Spirit.

I slowly approached the end of the city street where Christ the King was located, then drove my car into and around the circular driveway shaded by massive maple and oak trees. Finding a space in which to park my car, I turned off the ignition and got out. I turned around and stared. Before me stood a large brick structure which was to be my home for the next week. My gaze proceeded upward in wonderment. I was awed by the obvious old age of the building with its white stone columns and enamored with the peaceful, quiet atmosphere that greeted me. This was a place of respite and renewal for sure.

As I made my way up the walk to the front door, a chorus of bird songs enveloped me. Butterflies flitted about, seeming to be frequent visitors in my life. *All is well here. I will be well here*, I thought. I knew I was in for an awesome experience.

Cautiously, I opened the solid wooden door. I was greeted by a pious looking woman and given directions to my room. There, I unpacked, placing some of my clothes in the simple wooden dresser and hanging others on the hooks available by the door. The single bed greeted me along with a night stand. I placed the plant I had brought along on the desk near the single window as evidence of life, trust and hope for days ahead. I made up the bed, having brought my own sheets, blanket and pillow—plain, simple, basic. That was it . . . that was enough. Delightful.

I had gotten used to the cycle of emotions I experienced in my retreats. It took a day or two to familiarize myself with my surroundings, to find my "spaces", if you will, where I was comfortable to sit, meditate and write. Here, the serenity and peace allowed for many choices, and they might be different for different times of day. Of course, it was a time of getting to know my spiritual director whom I might have chosen from a list of unknowns. There was the building itself to familiarize myself with, and where things were located.

This crowded residential area of Syracuse is definitely a far cry from the natural stillness and beauty of Maria Renata on the shores of Lake Placid, I thought, chuckling, *yet, I can find peace and quiet almost anywhere. Peace in my inner world can* always *be there, if I choose to tap into it.* That was my first awareness on this retreat.

The beginning days dealt with present, ongoing issues in my life. Would I be delving into the issues surrounding my resignation from the parochial school? What about my failing marriage? What about the anger I felt or the betrayal that always clouded my emotions? So I patiently waited to be drawn to a focus.

On the third day of my retreat, I wandered off the grounds along a quiet residential street. *There, for the first time ever, I saw a cottonwood tree.* There were amazing puffy balls all over the sidewalk in front of me. There were also pieces of thin papery bark that had been shed in sheets everywhere. I stood there, awed. *Nature is truly a marvel,* I thought.

Then I saw it. A nest had fallen out of the tree, having been battered by wind and rain. I walked over to where it rested and slowly bent over, gently picking up the configuration of twigs and bark and grass. "This was once a home, a nest for baby birds," I said aloud.

I felt my eyes squeezing shut and tears filling them. Suddenly I knew what I was being drawn to deal with. It was the little one I had lost August 8, 1986. It was now July 28, 1992. *It's been six years.*

All at once, to my surprise, a wave of deep pain surged from within. I doubled over and let the sudden tears flow. Grief and guilt that I had locked away gripped my insides. I allowed the pain and felt the descent into the bottom of my soul.

There I stayed, in that place of loss and pain, allowing myself to feel yet a deeper level of grief that, for some reason,

I'd never allowed myself to feel, and certainly had not expected to encounter today.

After a time, I felt a slow leveling off begin. As I struggled to take a deep breath, I opened my eyes and slowly looked down at the nest which still rested in the palm of my hand. I carried it gently as I moved back to the retreat grounds, searching for a place where I could rest and quietly speak to my little one, Kari Rose, and listen to her message. I recorded these thoughts in my journal.

July 29,

Kari Rose, I long to speak with you, to touch you, to hold you and to feel your arms around my neck. I want to hug you. I want to see the mischievousness in your eyes and the delight. I want to feel your presence and your love.

You don't blame me, do you? I'm sorry I haven't remembered your anniversary every year and that does shame me. I get caught up in your sisters and your dad and doing all I'm called to and I forget you, my precious one. Forgive me, please forgive me. Let me know you forgive me so I can forgive myself.

I have many times felt your presence. I love you, my little one, with all my heart. Help me now. If you were here, I'd be helping you, but, instead, I'm asking for your help.

We can talk . . . and the next time I make cookies, I won't really be alone, will I? I haven't been alone but I forgot and didn't recognize your presence.

Thank you for your help in my healing after I was diagnosed and as I went through my mom's passing.

Glory be to God, YOU ARE REAL and I haven't treated you so. Take care.

I love you,

Mother

As I wrote these thoughts, I felt such shame because I *hadn't* thought of her in such a long time. I experienced that wonderful shame that Mom convinced me of so long ago—that I was a bad person. The butterfly that I had caught and that had died was my earliest memory of her reprimand. *Would I never be rid of the shame of it all?* I guessed it was still there, festering.

Mom, I'm here. You haven't lost me. I'll always be here, not far away at all. I hear your words and feel your smile. I'm happy and peaceful. That would be important for you to know. I love you, Mom, and about forgiveness, there is nothing to forgive. I understand, you know. I understand.

Rest peacefully, Mom. Sleep gently. And the next time you make cookies, I'll be there watching!

Your precious one,

Kari Rose

I felt such deep, deep sadness after her sharing. So many

tears poured down my face. The message was forgiveness, forgive those who have offended me. By my not forgiving her dad for not being present to me during the miscarriage and my diagnosis, *I* was blocking my being able to forgive myself. That was another awareness of this retreat.

I gave in to the weariness I was feeling and stretched out on the grass by the pool. Resting my head on my folded arms, I closed my eyes. I began to drift off, feeling a peaceful presence.

Upon awakening, I sat up and immediately put pen to paper as if Kari Rose had inspired another message to me. And so she had:

> *I had to die, Mommy. I have a special mission—to help you carry the burdens of others' feelings.*
>
> *If I were a living child you could hold, I wouldn't understand you as I do now and couldn't help you with your special grace. Most people never reach the depths you can go, Mommy, and just as you can hurt so deeply, you can experience that depth of joy.*
>
> *Be at peace, Mom. You shall always be my mother.*
>
> *You and I will travel together. You are not alone and remember, I understand.*
>
> > *Your precious one,*
> >
> > *Kari Rose*

As I put down my pen, I realized my cheeks were wet with tears for I had just been given a precious gift, the gift of understanding. The guilt I had carried these six years for not being delighted with the pregnancy had begun to melt away. The shame I had felt over not having remembered my child's anniversary of her death had begun to melt away, too.

Now I *understood* why it had all happened, why it *had* to happen, but I knew it would take time to completely understand the healing that had taken place.

And, intuitively, I knew. "Kari Rose" means "gentle flower". What a gift I had just received.

But, can I really believe her words? Can I really forgive myself, *allow* myself forgiveness? There was that doubt again creeping in. It was going to take time, a lot of time. My history of not being able to forgive myself was long and filled with deep emotion.

I felt engulfed in the feelings generating from my miscarriage and loss. It dominated my mind and all the feelings running through me. I labored between wanting to believe her words and being overcome with the recurring guilt and shame that I had lived with for so long.

I remembered how my so-called friends avoided the topic of my having had a miscarriage, how few expressed words of comfort. It was as if nothing had happened, as if I hadn't lost my child.

If Kari Rose *had* been born and *then* died, many people would have expressed their sympathy. But in the case of a miscarriage, that group support isn't always there. At least it wasn't for *me*.

No one spoke about it. My husband didn't want to even share what *he* was feeling or going through himself. This told me that her life was not of the same value as a birthed child in their minds. And yet, to *me,* it certainly was.

There was one card that I *did* receive. It was from someone I hardly knew. She shared about having had her own miscarriage. I felt such comradery with her, her words coming from a heart filled with empathy. That's when I realized that empathy was what I so desired—empathy, not sympathy. And so I continued to grieve.

As I continued my retreat, I still found myself struggling with the fact that I had to give my permission for the D & C. The fetus might still have had a heartbeat. I might have killed my own baby. My body might have still been hanging onto the pregnancy. All these fears and doubts sought to overwhelm me.

I read Kari's words to me over and over but I still couldn't quite give up the thought that it was all somehow my fault. The self-blame began to weigh me down.

I took my journal with me everywhere, even to our silent meals, in case I sensed her presence and she sought to communicate. Finally, it happened late the following day.

I was sitting in one of my "quiet" places and felt the urge to journal. The words came without thought, a sure sign that it was Kari Rose. With pen to paper, I wrote without stopping. Only *then* did I read her message and try to understand it.

> *July 30*
>
> *Mommy, you had to give permission. My Father's will be done. It was the way it had to be. That was why you consecrated me to God on that bike ride the day before my miscarriage began.*

Remember?

With a heart full of love and abandonment to God's will you said, 'I consecrate this child to You, Father, to do with as You will.' Remember? It was the way it had to be. Don't you see? You didn't say, 'Kill her' to the doctor.

You said you felt God carrying you throughout and so He did.

I was never in pain, Mommy. I was carried in the blood that left your womb to my haven in Heaven, to peace and love and joy. Thank you, Mommy, for giving me up and not holding on.

I love you, Mommy.

I knew I needed to trust in her words, her forgiveness. I needed to feel God's forgiveness. I knew I mustn't try to control how much she loved me, by thinking I didn't deserve it, but allow myself to *feel* her love. I felt more of the guilt and shame surrounding my miscarriage fading away. And I knew it was possible to feel free of it for once in my life.

I floated through the rest of my day, feeling a warmth and relaxation I rarely experienced. It had been a difficult few days but the experiences were necessary for my growth. *Where will I grow from here?* I wondered. My retreat wasn't over yet. There were still a few days left.

The following night, my sleep was deep. In the morning, I awoke with a start. I was anxious and trembling. Blood! Blood was everywhere! *Where am I? What's happening?*

Then another scene flashed through my mind. There was

blood flowing out of my own wrists, both of them. Awareness took over. *My soul is dying. My soul is dying.* Over and over, I repeated those words. *What did they mean? What* could *they mean? How could my soul be dying? I feel okay.*

I was in a panic. I was sweating profusely. My heart was racing and pounding so forcefully that I thought I might be forced back down on my bed by its strength. It was then that I realized I was sitting up in my bed. My breathing was coming in short raspy gasps, my whole body rigid.

Suddenly, I fell backward onto my pillow. I could still feel my heart racing as I tried, with little success, to quiet myself. I felt like I had been in a nightmare.

As I lay there, staring at the ceiling, I began to concentrate on slowing my breathing with much fuller, deeper breaths. I could feel my heart as it began to quiet and my muscles let go of their tension. But all that blood had left a lasting impression, a stain on my mind.

I slowly sat up again and grabbed for my pen and journal. Having signed up for the earlier Dream Workshop, I had now followed it with an eight-day retreat. The woman who had conducted the workshop was my spiritual director.

I had learned that if upon waking from a dream we are experiencing some emotion like fear, sadness, horror, uneasiness, joy or peace, we are to write down as much detail as possible about the dream and discuss it with our spiritual director. So, I began to write.

The day seemed to progress quite slowly as I anxiously awaited the scheduled time for my meeting. This was going to be an exceptional session.

As I walked into the room, journal in hand, Judy greeted me as always with her warm, friendly, encouraging smile. She was an intuitive, compassionate woman of prayer who had cried with me during our first meeting as I spoke with her of the deep pain I experienced in my marriage. No one had ever cried with me before and it had touched me deeply. *Could this dream have something to do with my marriage?* I wondered.

Upon listening to my detailed account of the dream, she asked, "How did you feel upon awakening?"

"Scared to death."

"Tell me how you felt *physically*," she requested.

"My heart was racing, my muscles were all tense and I was sweating," I answered.

"Our blood is mostly water, and water is life-giving," she explained, "and sometimes it represents life in our dreams."

"So I'm losing my life?" I inquired with a puzzled look on my face. "How? I feel okay."

"Maybe not literally losing your life, but possibly your spirit is dying."

Suddenly, I knew what the dream meant. I had no doubt. "My soul is dying by staying in my marriage," I said with conviction. "But I can't leave. What about the girls?"

"I don't have answers to your questions," she told me, "but just like in the case of your miscarriage, I think the time will come when you will *know* the answers. Spend time praying and writing. Keep your heart open and loving."

I had the slightest sensation that I *did* know one answer,

but I wouldn't let myself acknowledge it or accept it. *Could it possibly be that staying in my marriage was destroying my soul? How could that be?*

I felt very confused and decided to shove that thought back to the furthest recesses of my mind. I was not going to dwell on it. Instead, I let the renewed feeling I had felt concerning my miscarriage creep to the forefront. I felt the warm love of Kari Rose envelop me.

I had been allowed that deep healing experience with Kari Rose, maybe to help prepare me for the next step on my journey. Maybe having *that* experience had then allowed a *deeper* awareness to rise to the surface, an awareness which I would, at some time, need to deal with.

Well, I would return to my home renewed, a little more at peace, a little more patient, a bit more loving, and with a lingering issue I was not ready to acknowledge. Yet, my positive nature left me filled with hope for the future.

Focusing on the positive, I welcomed the approach of fall, my favorite season. Enjoying the array of colors, the aroma of fallen leaves, and the quieting down of Nature, I prepared for the blanketing of winter.

The winter of 1992 had arrived with snow crystals every-where, glistening in the light of day like sparkling diamonds. Windows which were covered with the creeping frost of night gave way to streamlets of water by day. I spent much of my time in Nature, cross-country skiing in the woods, letting time and silence effect my healing.

I still saw a spiritual director once a month, though he was not the original one I had started with. Insights flooded my mind and my journaling increased.

Along with spring came a renewal within me as Nature budded forth.

One day, I was working among my flowers, humming softly to myself as I so often did. As I reached to snip a blossom, a scene flashed through my mind. I was frozen by the possibility of it all. I slowly began to stand, aghast at the scene I had just witnessed in my mind. I moved as if in a daze.

"No! No!" I exclaimed. "I can't let that happen."

The scene was clear as a bell as it ran through my mind again and again. I saw each and every person clearly and succinctly.

My husband's parents were the main characters in my scene with all the same tension between them that they usually demonstrated. They were one unhappy couple, stuck in the world they had created with each other.

Besides that, life had dealt them many blows which sought to make them bitter toward each other. Job loss had hounded his dad along with some poor life choices and he had sought drink as his main coping mechanism, not only for the stresses he lived with, but also to buoy up a disintegrating self-image. The result was alcoholism. His wife had become his enabler, sharing a drink with him regularly. They were good people with a fine sense of humor but so unhappy with each other.

Then, in a flash, I had seen my husband and myself many years from now, just as stuck and as miserable as his parents were then. I knew at that moment, that this was the way it *could* turn out and *would* turn out, if something didn't change soon.

It was then that my focus began to shift. It wasn't what *I* could no longer tolerate. It was the treatment I didn't want my girls to *have* to tolerate from their future partners, thinking that such treatment was normal and acceptable. It was unloving and anything *but* normal. The dysfunction would be perpetuated. I couldn't pretend anymore that all was okay. I knew I had to leave my marriage.

But how? And when? My faith and intuition told me that I would know, just as Sister Judy had said during my silent retreat. And it wouldn't be long. The knowing held no doubts for me now. I knew for certain. My marriage was over.

There was nothing more I could try to do, nothing more I could forgive. Our couple's counseling had not resulted in changes.

"If you're not happy, that's *your* problem," my husband told me. "I'm fine." Obviously, this was not something *we* were going to work on together.

The Myers-Briggs Personality Inventory indications had only given him an excuse for *not* working on change.

"That's the way I am," he said flatly.

Individual counseling had begun to show some progress in our relationship, yet, when the counselor left the area, my husband didn't seek another as a replacement.

"I'm fine," he replied, in answer to my query.

My leaving was imminent.

What will my sisters and brother say? I wondered. Marriage was supposed to be for life. None of my friends in high school or college had divorced parents. My religious instruction told me that it was wrong to divorce. *How can I do it?* I queried. *But I must . . . somehow.*

My thoughts wandered back to my last retreat. Maybe the greatest awareness I had gained was my becoming attuned to the fact that my physically *dead* child, who lives on as spirit, and has given me such grace, was helping me to feel so *alive*. While contrarily, the marriage which still existed *now* was causing the *death* of my soul.

I became aware of a presence, a spiritual presence.

I felt an overwhelming sense of gentleness, a kindness and an exceedingly deep love being poured out on me. Somehow I knew it was my mom. She was lending me strength, *her* strength. She was with me in my leaving. I was not alone. She wasn't able to leave *her* marriage as miserable as she was in it but she would help me to leave mine.

I felt her approval. It meant the world to me. I felt her love for me as I had never felt while growing up.

"Okay, Mom," I cried. "Help me."

I needed to decide on yet another *first step*. It seemed as though my life were made up of a conglomeration of first steps. Once that step was taken, however, other steps followed in sequence, sometimes without my noticing. That first step brought the greatest challenge and this time was no different.

Though I had a Master's Degree in Science, I didn't have a full-time teaching job. *I need to begin substitute teaching in the public school system again so that I can support myself and the girls*, I thought. *I can't do that in our town because everyone knows that I have MS. It has to be elsewhere.* I felt myself being drawn to another even smaller community thirty miles away.

And so it was that I applied and was accepted at Long Lake Central School. I was called there to substitute most days of the week and I loved it. The staff was appreciative and supportive and even requested my presence over and over. Much to my surprise, they *did* know of my diagnosis and still they called. I was included in all the faculty functions and grew in my self-confidence as a teacher as well as personally. They were a fine group of people with a great sense of humor.

It was there that I met my best friend. I had never understood the term *soul mate* until then.

It made me realize that I had never had a *best* friend, even in high school. And I wasn't allowed to have boys as friends. There had been people I'd admired but never someone I could share my feelings with openly without fear of condemnation. So when I did develop a friendship with a boy in college, I thought he was the one I was supposed to marry.

He asked and I said, "Yes," since I really liked him. He probably could have been a good friend for many years. But he was not a good choice as a spouse, at least not mine. "Yes," was my immaturity and inexperience talking. My two girls were the gifts of that relationship, though, and I would never in a million years regret that aspect of the marriage.

My *soul mate* was kind, supportive, fun, open and understanding. He was generous and loyal. I knew *he'd* defend me if there was ever a need, professionally or personally.

We spoke of death and of life, our ideas and our philosophies. We became spiritual partners. We spoke of our dreams—those we'd lost and those we still hoped to attain. We spoke of our struggles without criticism or condemnation. Our talking sessions went on for hours. If we disagreed, it was rare. We seemed to understand where each other was coming from and accepted that. Our talks took us to Nature and she became our sounding board and source of insight. She was our resource and our guide, helping us to put all things in perspective.

We were soul mates in the truest of terms.

We loved the same activities, some of which I'd never found anyone to share with before. And we both found healing in Nature. That was key for me. There was an *automatic* understanding of each other that I'd never experienced with another human being, male nor female. Being with him was like *coming home, coming home to a part of myself.*

And I hoped we'd be best friends for life.

In our society, it is difficult to be married and be best friends with someone other than your spouse. Other people do not understand that relationship, nor are they willing to accept it. I had no romantic feelings at the time. I reveled in the feeling that I could *just be myself,* for once in my life.

I thoroughly enjoyed the students, K–12, and subbed at anything and everything. By the time the year was over, I had experienced teaching the entire student body. I was happy there.

At home, my marriage continued disintegrating. It was as if my husband felt threatened by the growth he saw happening within me and the happiness I carried home with me each day from Long Lake.

As my self-image grew, I began speaking up and not accepting his critical comments. Resentment and unhappiness grew until the *how* to leave and *when* to leave became clear.

I remained focused on the girls and my commitment to their knowing they need not remain in a degrading relationship in their adult lives. Hopefully, they would *not* make their choices of mates based on how they saw my husband treating *me*. They deserved better. I did not want them to stay stuck in a relationship that was not supportive and encouraging.

There is always *choice*.

15

AN ENDING

Where had my journey of awareness begun? When had that spark been ignited, allowing me to grow in understanding myself and possibly even accept the belief that I was okay?

It had all started with the Myers-Briggs Personality Inventory which I had taken years ago. Sister Catherine had worked with me in interpreting what it had shown. These were my gifts. There were no negatives. *How could that be?* I wondered. *Aren't there always negatives, answers that are incorrect or show weaknesses and failures?*

She assured me not.

The inventory showed that I was a strong introvert, meaning that I had to think before speaking as compared to an extrovert who speaks *to* think. We all possess some of both qualities but function mainly in one area which becomes our strength.

I'd always felt uncomfortable in groups when others were volunteering. I couldn't just jump in. Now I knew why.

I had never liked discussion groups, either. Besides having little confidence in my ideas or opinions, I needed to think through the posed propositions. The whole discussion might be over before I formulated my thoughts.

I also needed peace and quiet to rejuvenate. People and populated places wore me out quickly. In contrast, people who are extroverts get reenergized by groups and action.

So, I realized that both were acceptable. There were others who had qualities similar to mine. Introverts *are* in the minority of the total population. I had certainly *felt* in the minority most of my life.

Next, I found out that I was intuitive. The inventory indicated that this was my gift area. I had never understood all the sensations I'd get when I entered a room. I could feel the sadness, fear, anger, and sorrow that I knew wasn't mine, when all around me people were laughing and presumably having a good time. It had been a puzzling contradiction for me much of my life. Those who exhibited extra-sensory perception or who were clairvoyant had a high intuitive score, too.

The inventory helped me to see that my ability to pick up on others' feelings, and sometimes even their thoughts, was a positive quality instead of "impossible," as my husband had many times indicated. I began to be intrigued by the future sensations I would discern.

The Meyers-Briggs showed me that I was a feeler as opposed to a thinker, meaning that I interpreted my world through my feelings more than through thought. This quality was also strong.

I realized that my crying with others who were showing emotion was due to this quality. I began to understand that I was a compassionate person and that this was positive. I no longer had to feel embarrassed when the tears began to flow. It was hard to ignore others' reactions when I dissolved into tears, but it got easier over time.

I realized that it was this quality that caused camaraderie with most people and it also extended to the world of Nature. I could feel pain in my arm as a live tree was being cut down. That was special.

My final quality was exercising judgment. I was a very organized person without even trying. I could organize in my mind quickly. I had lists for groceries and tasks needing to be done, and I was the household budgeter.

I could size up situations and decide on the best action. In that area, I needed to integrate other options so I didn't judge too quickly. My score showed that a bit more flexibility could be healthy for me. *That* I could manage. So what was the message? Slow down and take my time when making a decision. Things were not as black and white as I had previously thought. There were a lot of gray areas to consider.

After taking the inventory, I began to make some changes. Some were made consciously. Some crept in without my taking stock of them, but the results were there anyway, and I felt better about myself, little by little.

Awareness is a marvelous tool for initiating change and a necessary one for me.

I remembered the first time I became aware that I really had changed, at least in the practice of grocery shopping.

As I entered the grocery store, I pulled my list out of my pocket. Yes, I was an organized person and always would be.

I saw that as a gift. It would probably be some time before I didn't feel a twinge of guilt at buying groceries that weren't on sale, but I knew I'd get there.

At the top of my list was bread. I moved down the appropriate aisle, perused the varieties and selected some multigrain bread after carefully reading the ingredients. I wanted 100 percent whole grain in as natural a state as possible.

All of a sudden, I burst out laughing. *I can't believe I'm doing this,* I thought, grabbing a second loaf along with the first. *I'll store these in the freezer as backups to my homemade. There are times I can't make every loaf and I won't feel that ungodly pressure to do just that.* I fought the guilt that tried to take hold at the action I had just taken, as if I'd committed a crime. But I won! I wasn't going to do that to myself anymore.

I finished the rest of my shopping, checking my list carefully. I carted the bags to my car and got in.

The drive home was pleasant. I found myself humming a tune as I drove. I actually felt a little freer just from buying a few loaves of bread.

To me this little victory was amazing.

My heart felt light. I was on the right track.

As I danced through the front door of our home, my whole being felt lighter. It was as if I had unlocked a door within me that I hadn't realized was closed.

After I returned home and put away the groceries, my daughter scurried into the kitchen.

"Mom, do you have an empty jar I could use for a science project?"

"Sure," I answered. "There's a box of jars in the coat closet."

"Great!"

She quickly ran out. I could hear her yank open the closet door. Then there was a sharp clanking sound followed by the clattering echo of falling objects.

"Wow, which one should I take?"

"Well, what size do you need?" I replied as I turned to leave the kitchen.

Rounding the corner, my eyes took in the sight. There she was, sitting among an array of glass jars of various shapes and sizes. Some were upright and some were lying on their sides. Some were clear, some brown, still others were green in color.

A chuckle began bubbling up inside me until it erupted into a genuine laugh. She joined in as I flopped down on the carpeted floor beside her.

"You really have a lot of jars, Mom."

"Yes, I guess I do. Well, it'll be easy to pick out the one you want." And our laughter again erupted. "I think it's time to get rid of most of them. What do you think?"

"Can we recycle them?" she asked.

"Of course. I'll save just a few. They're handy to use for extra milk and juice, but I guess I don't need *all* of these," I said, still chuckling. *What had I been thinking?* The innocence of children had made me realize the extreme to which I had previously gone, saving *every* jar. A change was overdue.

Again months passed, and I witnessed the approach of fall with its spectacle of yellows, oranges and reds. Even the tamaracks had turned their characteristic golden yellow late in the season. It was like a four act play, each species peaking with its scene, on cue.

Many anniversaries and birthdays of family and friends were strewn throughout the fall like so many leaves upon the ground. I needed to organize my cards.

"Has anyone seen the box of notecards I picked up last week?" I called to the girls.

"Try the desk drawer, Mom," my youngest yelled from her room.

Walking over to the desk, I pulled open the drawer. I paused as realization struck. I was actually considering sending out some *purchased* cards along with my own handmade ones this year.

The sense of guilt began to descend. I felt my heart sink, as I had so often experienced.

And then the descent abruptly halted. *Wait a minute. It's the thought that counts. My own words written in a notecard would be meaningful, too, and I wouldn't be putting myself under the old performance pressure to create them* all. Then and there I decided to create my own for close family and to send the others to nonfamily members.

The amazing thing was that I consciously felt my shoulders relax and my heart slow its beat. I hadn't realized I'd been holding my breath during my dilemma. Maybe I was finally beginning to relax in that arena where I'd always felt driven. Before I'd felt like I had to do more and more, or do it better and better.

I was never satisfied with the result. My heart would feel clutched and my shoulder and neck muscles would be tight as bark on a tree. Now, I could feel myself beginning to relax as I identified my areas of stress. I *was* changing. I could see it, and what was even more important was that I could *feel* it.

It was time again for a checkup with my primary care physician. He always gave me the same evaluation after my retreat.

"Each time you return from your silent retreats, I find you have achieved an even deeper level of peace than the previous year." *Why was that? How had I gotten here?*

I knew that my physical symptoms had gradually abated over these past few years. My left hand had eventually recovered much of its muscle tone. That was aided by my squeezing a dense rubber ball a few times in a row each day, gradually building up to one hundred times in one session, as recommended by my doctor.

My left leg had improved also, hesitating only when I was tired. Then I would find myself tripping over the smallest root in the path or stone on the driveway. I attribute much of that improvement to my persistence at bicycle riding a little each day, upward of a few miles. Four was the most I could do on a "good day" at that time.

A "good day" was defined as when my energy levels allowed for it. I believe the B-Complex and Vitamin C capsules I'd begun taking, to aid my immune and nervous systems in dealing with stress, were making a difference.

I had been helped with identifying my stressors at that time by attending some workshops offered by Barbara Walker and her Consortium of People Educators (COPE) presentations. I spent time doing the activities she suggested and worked through many thoughtful questions. Answering these questions helped me to see how others' expectations of me affected me. I also began to learn how to use assertiveness in dealing with people without giving the impression of aggressiveness.

Then there was that inner voice of degradation and recrimination that persisted in adding to my declining self-image. I found I had a choice. I didn't *have* to listen to what that voice was telling me if it was degrading, telling me I was a failure. Instead, I began to speak up, proclaiming that I wasn't a failure. I had simply made a mistake, which happens to everyone. I made a conscious effort not to judge myself so harshly.

Only my husband could bring me down with a roll of his eyes, a certain look of disgust, or a critical verbal comment. It became more and more evident to me how incompatible we were.

Gradually my self-image had begun to grow to a level where I began to rise above his comments, noting them but not allowing them to bring me down.

I began to discuss my stressors with my primary care physician. In one of our discussions, he noted that I seem to admire certain qualities that others exhibit and then *expect* to possess all of these qualities, which is impossible. Since I don't possess them, I feel as if I'm a failure.

So, I asked myself, why was I working so hard at acquiring *all* of these qualities and expecting it was *possible* for me to acquire them all? I never seemed to be happy with myself. How could I be? I was attempting the impossible, setting myself up for failure every time.

Maybe a healthier way of approaching this dilemma was to pick out one quality I admired and honestly evaluate myself. If I found there was room for improvement, then I could incorporate more opportunities to exercise that quality. And, honestly, if I were lacking in that quality altogether, was it something I valued *enough* to promote change, or could I accept that it just wasn't a quality I had?

Something else my doctor commented on surfaced during our discussion of foods and sugars. I was strictly a no refined sugar person, something which none of my friends agreed with. He threw out this perspective for me to consider.

"Have you ever thought that *you* are the one who's right and *they* are wrong?"

"No. But could that be true?"

"*I* think so," he replied.

It was true that I had always thought everyone else knew more than I did. It was like my mom's comment, "Don't turn out dumb like me." I realized that, over the years, I had taken on that same attitude. So, not only did everyone else *know* more but they were always *right*, too, at least in *my* mind.

I became a bit more observant of my thought processes, adopting the inkling that I *could* be right in my opinions and practices at least some of the time, especially concerning my nutritional philosophy.

In addition to identifying some of my causes of stress and working on adapting some behaviors and practices, I noticed I was also becoming more flexible in accepting others' opinions and attitudes. I realized how rigid my thinking had become in certain areas and I began to loosen up. I realized that *accepting* the opinion of someone else was not the same as *agreeing* with it. The two *could* co-exist.

For many years I had tried to concentrate on the good I saw in people, not their flaws. I had felt put down, ridiculed and humiliated, and I didn't want to convey that feeling to others.

Maybe the only way to make me stop and see what I was doing to myself was to temporarily inhibit my being able to move physically, increasing my overall awareness. The physical arena *had* become the basis for my identity, not what was *within* me, the person I had grown to be. Had the MS been allowed, to give me the opportunity to *choose* growth and positive change? The other choice was to remain resistant, stuck and miserable. I was a positive person, usually, so I figured growth was the way to go, wherever it might lead me.

I began to allow my tears to flow freely, without the previous feeling of embarrassment. I began to see them as the so-called "gift of tears". They were a blessing to be grateful for, and I was grateful.

I knew it wouldn't happen overnight, but I had begun to let go of having to do and redo to make something *perfect*. I had been wasting a lot of time and energy on skewed expectations. It's difficult for a perfectionist to accept being less than perfect. *Maybe I need to modify my view of what perfect is,* I thought.

As I adapted my making and doing *everything,* I became more secure and more assertive. I felt the emotional healings that I had experienced during my silent retreats had coincided with spiritual growth. Facing the demons I had carried for years freed my body to use its energy to heal me physically.

The paramount emotion for me was forgiveness. There was a lot of forgiving I had needed to do. I knew it wasn't over yet, but I was more peaceful inside, as my physician had observed.

I began speaking up, taking ownership of my feelings and not accepting my husband's ridicule of them. They were *not* ridiculous. They were *not* wrong. They were mine and mine alone.

Whenever I had listed what my negative stressors were, I knew my marriage was a big one. Still, I had persisted in pushing that aside for many years, hoping it would improve. I didn't know what else I could do to effect progress in our marriage. I had exhausted my list of things to try, things to work on.

Whitney Houston had a recording out at the time called "The Greatest Love of All". I had played it daily, first after I had received my diagnosis and then any time I felt my world tumbling down around me.

The Greatest Love of All
(lyrics by Linda Creed, music by Michael Masser, produced by Michael Masser)

I believe the children are our future
Teach them well and let them lead the way
Show them all the beauty they possess inside
Give them a sense of pride to make it easier
Let the children's laughter remind us how we
 used to be

Everybody searching for a hero
People need someone to look up to
I never found anyone to fulfill my needs
A lonely place to be
So I learned to depend on me
I decided long ago

Never to walk in anyone's shadows
If I fail, if I succeed
At least I will live as I believe
No matter what they take from me
They can't take away my dignity

Chorus:
Because the greatest love of all
Is happening to me
I found the greatest love of all
Inside of me
The greatest love of all
Is easy to achieve
Learning to love yourself
It is the greatest love of all

I believe the children are our future
Teach them well and let them lead the way
Show them all the beauty they possess inside
Give them a sense of pride to make it easier
Let the children's laughter remind us how we
used to be

And I decided long ago
Never to walk in anyone's shadows
If I fail, if I succeed
At least I live as I believe
No matter what they take from me
They can't take away my dignity

Chorus:
Because the greatest love of all
Is happening to me
I found the greatest love of all
Inside of me
The greatest love of all
Is easy to achieve
Learning to love yourself
It is the greatest love of all

And if by chance, that special place
That you've been dreaming of
Leads you to a lonely place
*Find your strength in love**

I coupled that experience with listening to "Hero" by Mariah Carey.

Hero

(written and produced by Mariah Carey and Walter Afanasieff)

There's a hero
If you look inside yourself
You don't have to be afraid
Of what you are
There's an answer
If you reach into your soul
And the sorrow that you know
Will melt away
And then a hero comes along

With the strength to carry on
And you cast your fears aside
And you know you will survive
So when you feel like hope is gone
Look inside you and be strong
And you'll finally see the truth
That a hero lies in you

It's a long road
When you face the world alone
No one reaches out a hand
For you to hold
You can find love
If you search within yourself
And the emptiness you felt
Will disappear

And then a hero comes along
With the strength to carry on
And you cast your fears aside
And you know you will survive
So when you feel like hope is gone
Look inside you and be strong
And you'll finally see the truth
That a hero lies in you

Lord knows
Dreams are hard to follow
But don't let anyone

Take them away
Hold on
There will be tomorrow
In time
You'll find the way

And then a hero comes along
With the strength to carry on
And you know you can survive
So when you feel like hope is gone
Look inside you and be strong
And you'll finally see the truth
*That a hero lies in you***

Both would give me a boost for my day. Lying on the floor of my living room with my eyes closed, I could feel myself absorbing strength and courage by listening to the words and music.

Now it was with me constantly as a daily meditation. I gave voice to the words. I would catch myself humming the musical notes.

---

* ** Both songs can be listened to online under the singers' names. The voices and the music create an atmosphere I found very enveloping, inspiring and for me, quite healing deep, deep, down.

I also read a book which began to change my life—*Learning To Love Yourself* by Sharon Wegscheider-Cruse. Besides her discussions of guilt and shame and other emotions we encounter, she suggested some methods we can use to help improve our belief in ourselves. One jumped out at me.

So, I wrote ten positive qualities about myself on an index card and taped it in a place I often visited throughout the day. For me, that was my bedroom mirror.

1. *I like my smile.*
2. *I like my determination.*
3. *I like my sense of humor.*
4. *I like my sensitivity.*
5. *I like my intuition.*
6. *I like the fact that I'm not fat*
7. *I like my body*
8. *I like my gift of loving to give to people*
9. *I like my gift of dance.*
10. *I like my ability to budget.*

Each day I read those qualities many times, sometimes out loud, and gradually that mantra began to replace some of my negative head talk. After a few weeks I found I began to recognize other positives about myself, too. I replaced the notecard with another, listing different qualities I saw and again a third time. It worked.

I realized that since two objects could not occupy the same space at the same time, neither could two thoughts. Thinking positive thoughts replaced the negative ones. I was on my way.

My youth had been so lacking in the building of a healthy self-image, self-pride and self-confidence. I therefore grew to feel insecure, doubtful, unsafe, unloved, of little value—in a nutshell, worthless. Yet, on some level, I knew I was special. I had set my goals and accomplished some things. I had tried to find the positive in the negative things that were happening around me, and I had focused on providing my daughters with what had been so lacking, emotionally, in my own upbringing.

I was trying to grow, identify my causes of stress and change what I could to help myself, but I couldn't change my husband or make *him* grow. Only *he* could do that. Only *he* could see the need to do that.

In his own words, "You grow in leaps and bounds, and I don't grow at all."

By coming to understand myself more and nurturing a better self-image, I felt I was contributing a lot to our crumbling relationship, in the hopes of saving it. I didn't see my husband putting forth the same effort, if any.

His previous comment, "If you're not happy, it's *your* problem," said it all. He did not see himself as a contributing factor.

So where was I to go? What options did I have left?

When substituting at Long Lake for the high school English teacher, I had opened a book of poetry which I had found on his desk. There on the page was a poem by Edgar Lee Masters entitled, "Mrs. Charles Bliss." I made a copy. It provided me with more affirmation for what I was about to finalize.

Mrs. Charles Bliss

Reverend Wiley advised me not to divorce him
For the sake of the children,
And Judge Somers advised him the same
So we stuck to the end of the path.
But two of the children thought he was right,
And two of the children thought I was right.
And the two who sided with him blamed me,
And the two who sided with me blamed him,
And they grieved with the one they sided with.
And all were torn with the guilt of judging,
And tortured in soul because they could not admire
Equally him and me.
Now every gardener knows that plants grown in cellars
Or under stones are twisted and yellow and weak.
And no mother would let her baby suck
Diseased milk from her breast.
Yet preachers and judges advise the raising of souls
Where there is no sunlight, but only twilight,
No warmth, but only dampness and cold—
Preachers and judges!

The awareness of my last retreat came back to me, loud and clear.

My soul is dying. If I stayed in this marriage, I accepted the death of my spirit, but I had so much inside yet to discover and share. I *knew* that. There really wasn't another choice left to me. To stay was death.

I choose life!

My hope was that this action which I needed to take would kick-start some growth for my husband, in addition to helping prevent some strife in the future for my daughters. In pain we have a choice—grow through it or remain floundering in it.

I knew he could be happier.

Maybe my marriage had been a wrong turn or maybe it was *necessary* in order for me to see what I was doing to myself, to my very soul, but that turn allowed me to be gifted with the raising and guiding of two special souls on *their* journeys. *That* I will *never* regret.

I began seeing a counselor who had been recommended by a lawyer I had seen to find out the process of separation. With the counselor, I began sharing background, and I asked her to be with me as I left my marriage.

In her wisdom she made a few comments I remember still.

"I don't think you ever *became* married," was one that gave me much food for thought. Another was that in her experience, she knew of a number of well-adjusted adults who were from divorced homes. It made me feel a great deal better. The girls could come through this and eventually be emotionally healthy adults. She emphasized that my main concern didn't need to be what the girls were having for supper at their father's, but what I needed to do to take care of myself.

And her final comment was this: "You are not leaving your girls. You are leaving your husband." That became my litany.

She was my sounding board, my guide, my support, my partner in sorrow and my inspiration.

With her support, I began taking the final steps to leave my marriage.

Leaving a marriage is neither easy nor without pain. Closing the door on the dreams of a lifetime of happiness with a particular person is nothing short of heart-wrenching. But there are times in our lives when we KNOW the path we are to take. Sometimes something we've been taught is *wrong* feels so *right*, and we need to go. For me it meant leaving a marriage of twenty-three years.

As the day neared for us to part, my husband said to me, "Now I know how lonely you've been all these years."

Yes, very lonely . . . indeed.

This has been *my* story and no one else's. We certainly *had* been emotionally unsuited to each other, two entirely different people, the wrong puzzle pieces trying over and over again to fit together.

I felt I was closing the book on a chapter of my life. But what of the chapters to come?

And what would happen with my Multiple Sclerosis? Would it rear its ugly head again?

Where would life lead me?

There were so many unanswerable questions running through my mind. I took a deep breath and slowly emptied my lungs. As I did, I knew that I was ridding myself of what no longer served me.

And I would be *okay.*

EPILOGUE

We are made up of so many emotional layers and those emotional layers can poison us and shape our future. I needed to peel those layers, so much like phyllo dough, layer by layer, to allow my body the energy to begin to heal itself. It has been hard work, painful work, but it's all been worth it. I have become a better person for it all, and much more genuine. I'm enjoying getting to know who I am.

Life is a journey and for me it's a journey of discovery, each and every day. And I am grateful, indeed, for the opportunity to pursue that mission.

As I discover more of who I am, I never cease to be amazed at the gifts I've uncovered. None of that would have been possible while I carried all of my emotional baggage.

I needed to face some of my demons, to be willing to experience the depth of pain that reliving a hurtful experience awakens in us, then move through it and rise out of it, a bit more aware, a bit more forgiving, a bit more loving. I'm ready to use my gifts and discover new ones that I never knew I possessed. This all coincided with a deep spiritual growth and physical healing.

We cannot segregate the emotional, spiritual and physical realms. They are intricately interwoven. If we can keep all three in balance, we prosper in phenomenal ways that we cannot even imagine. And that's the trick—balance.

How can we keep ourselves balanced?

For me it takes daily effort, awareness, and listening to my body. It will let me know what it needs and what it doesn't. If I treat my body with the respect it deserves, it will continue trying to heal itself.

As I moved through the final act of leaving my marriage, I knew there were more discovery and growth to come, along with healing of the effects my demons had had on me.

Leaving my marriage was an ending, but an ending with new beginnings on the horizon and so much yet to be learned.

But that's another story, the details of which are yet to be written.

Life is a journey and I'm so glad I'm now an *active* traveler. Previously, I was existing.

Now

    I

        Am

            Living.

AUTHOR'S NOTES

Writing this manuscript required my reliving each painful episode described herein and in so doing, I have finally put them to rest. That was a pleasant surprise for me. Through Nature, these effects have dissipated to the ethereal world. Never again has any of these episodes evoked a feeling of sadness, regret, shame or pain. They are only memories.

Healing my emotional traumas has had an amazingly positive effect on the Multiple Sclerosis I have lived with for many years. I now see my disease as a blessing, for it has opened many doors which I don't believe would have been opened while I was still driving myself to *do* it all perfectly and to *be* what someone else wanted me to be.

The emotional, physical and spiritual realms are indeed interwoven into one amazing Universe. From my experience I can say—

Healings are within our reach!

SPECIAL THANKS

To David Hazard, my writing and publishing coach. My
sincere thank you for all your patience, support,
encouragement and expertise. Words cannot thank
you enough.

To Wende Carr Woods for her editorial support. Thank
you for all your suggestions and proof-reading of
this manuscript. You've helped me to understand
a great deal.

To my readers (Elaine Baker, John Collins, Lynn Edmonds,
Karen Rappaport, Bronwyn Seal, Dan Sullivan).
Your truthful and sincere reactions to this manuscript were greatly appreciated as were your
explanations of how the reading of *my* story
affected you, personally. You gave me the final
impetus to bring this project to fruition.

To my daughters and grandchildren for being such a special
part of my life. I am honored to have you along on
my journey. You buoyed me up when times seemed
to drag and provided me with much needed breaks
from the grind. I love you so much.

To my family and friends for their encouragement along
the way and who continue to believe in my journey, to my physicians for their committed care and

presence and to my spiritual directors over the years for their listening and guidance. I love you all.

To Kelly Lindsay for all your help in Soul Loss and Soul Retrieval and to Dan Sullivan for your constant support and expertise in keeping me "balanced".

To my soulmate and best friend, Gary, without whose support and understanding, this manuscript would never have been finished.

To the healing presence that Nature has always been for me. In you I truly find my Source.

To all the characters in my book for the part they have played in my growth journey, whether they were a positive or negative influence at the time. It has all been worth it.

I AM HAPPY TO BE ME.

AUTHOR'S BIO

Debby Havas resides in the Adirondack Mountains of northern New York. There she welcomes the peace and quiet of Nature for both healing and rejuvenation. Walking the trails on her property and climbing the small mountain there are among her delights, along with spending time with family. She views her mission as caretaker of her land and protector of the wildlife that inhabit the property.

Now, in her later years, she lends her experiences in teaching and those of being a stay-at-home Mom to her writing, making it both realistic and personal in a down-to-earth comfortable style.

Made in the USA
Middletown, DE
07 May 2017